Wandering
through Life

Also by Donna Leon

DONNA LEON

A MEMOIR

Wandering through Life

Atlantic Monthly Press
New York

Originally published in Great Britain in 2023 by Hutchinson Heinemann, an imprint of Penguin Random House UK.

Published simultaneously in Canada
Printed in the United States of America

First Grove Atlantic hardcover edition: September 2023

Typeset by Integra Software Services Pvt. Ltd, Pondicherry

Library of Congress Cataloging-in-Publication data is available for this title.

ISBN 978-0-8021-6158-1
eISBN 978-0-8021-6159-8

Atlantic Monthly Press
an imprint of Grove Atlantic
154 West 14th Street
New York, NY 10011

Distributed by Publishers Group West

groveatlantic.com

23 24 25 26   10 9 8 7 6 5 4 3 2 1

For Angela Hewitt

Contents

Part Three: Italy

Part Four: In the Mountains

Preface

Like most of the events in my life, the thought of assembling this book came to me accidentally. Some years ago, at a dinner in Venice, I sat next to a person with whom I'd worked in Iran, and as we chatted about friends we had met while there, friends with whom we were still in contact, and then started to reminisce about some of the things we'd done, I had the chance to see them afresh. Because they'd been part of my daily life, I'd never thought that the events were particularly interesting. But then he made a casual reference to 'Armenian Circus' and, without a thought, we both crouched down on the floor and began to hop – with our much older knees – around the room like rabbits, much to the consternation of the other guests.

For the other people at dinner, it was obvious that we'd lost our minds. For us, however, this was the

main act of 'Armenian Circus', a game we'd played
with friends during the military curfew imposed on
the city of Isfahan, Iran, during the last few months I
spent working there in the late seventies. Of course,
we'd had costumes then, but they had not survived the
evacuation that took us from a violent Iran. Pity, really,
for they'd been made of great lengths of silk and an
inordinate number of feathers, and had made a great
contribution to the fun of the game.

The accompaniment had not been music but the
sound of machine-gun fire from the city and the occasional exploding bomb. The circus was a product of the
frequent pyjama parties that had resulted from the curfew imposed by both sides engaged in the Islamic
Revolution. Anyone seen on the street after 7 p.m. could
be shot. Many of us were in the habit of stopping to see
friends after work for a drink or a cup of tea, so we were
often stranded there by the wail of sirens that told us
we were going to have to sleep where we were and go
home after 6 a.m., when the curfew was lifted. Like
children shipwrecked on a magic island, we had to
invent ways to amuse ourselves – thus 'Armenian
Circus', though I no longer remember where the name
came from nor what the other parts of the game were.

As we tried to explain this to the people at the table,
to whom machine-gun fire was not the usual background noise at dinner, I realized that perhaps I had
seen and done unusual things.

I'd undertaken these things, I suspect, because I am
feckless and unthinking by nature and have never
planned more than the first step in anything I've done.
Take the first step – sign the contract, agree to the

interview, accept the job, rent the apartment – and then wait to see what could happen. *Something* has to happen, doesn't it? You might not know where you're going, but you have to end up *somewhere*, don't you?

2022 was my eightieth year, news that surprises even me, for at eighty, people are meant to be settled or in the process of settling. Unfortunately, the idea of settling in one place and doing one thing or – worse – not doing anything at all, has no appeal. The orchestra with which I work, Il Pomo d'Oro, has plans to record Handel's *Jephtha, Giulio Cesare, Berenice* and *Semele*, and that should keep me busy (and in vocal paradise) for some time. The casts and recording dates are as set as any dates can be in today's music world and so, like Handel's Semele, I am looking forward to 'endless pleasure'. I shall also have the opportunity to spend more time with Guido Brunetti, his family, and his friends and colleagues, and to give him the chance to reveal more about himself, his past, and what he thinks and feels.

Part One: America

1. Noll's Farm

My maternal grandfather, Joseph A. Noll, was born more than a hundred years ago in Nuremberg, Germany. And that's that. Well, it's that for anyone who wants more information about his origins. My other grandfather, Alberto de León, was born in Latin America, though he seems never to have mentioned which country. In fact, I have no memory of hearing either grandfather speak about the country in which he was born. It's as if they stepped off the boats, one as a German, the other as a citizen of that already forgotten country, and each set his foot down as an American.

Although neither of them had English as a native tongue, I never heard either of them speak a word in another language, and only my paternal grandfather had an accent. My German grandfather had been a farmer in Germany, and a farmer he became in Clifton, New Jersey.

He had thirty-five acres of land, and whenever I went there as a child to visit, it was paradise – no, Paradise.

There were, for starters, about fifty cows, two cold-blooded workhorses, Duke and Squire, my cousin's riding horse, a number of geese (mean as snakes), a heavy sprinkling of chickens, a few pigs, and a pair of ducks who, I was told, had stopped there while migrating, taken a look around, and decided to stay.

And about eight Irish workmen to care for and milk the cows. These workmen, I learned over the years, were transient. They lived on the farm, which was less than an hour from New York City, and worked hard all day, seven days a week. They were paid once a month, on the last day of the month, and that evening they disappeared. Two days later, whatever the day of the week, my grandfather drove his truck into New York City and down to the Bowery, known for its bars, flophouses, and brothels. He is said to have driven to a particular street corner, where he found his farmhands, much downtrodden, some still drunk, some with signs of having been in a fight, others missing a shoe or a jacket, or a tooth, all without a cent, and most of them much the worse for alcohol.

But they greeted my grandfather, it was said by my uncle Lawrence, who went on this monthly trip with him, with a mixture of gratitude and relief, and went back to the farm and back to work. For a month.

My brother and I were often at the farm, knew all of the farmhands, and were no doubt spoiled by some of them. Many had wives and children still in Ireland; some had younger brothers and sisters. My grandfather made it a condition of employment, I later learned, that they give him 25 per cent of their salaries, which he sent back to their families.

When I was about seven, we moved to a small house on the farm property and lived there for a year or so. It was there, I suppose, that I became familiar with the smell of the manure pile, which I still find aromatic rather than foul. I also saw the magic effect it had: every autumn the workers strewed it on the land, and every summer it showed the result.

Living there for a year let me see the entire work cycle. Planting corn and wheat in the spring, weeding it during the summer, scything the wheat and harvesting the corn in the fall.

Fall also brought the slaughter of the turkeys for Thanksgiving and, a month later, the Christmas slaughter. My grandfather sold the turkeys, along with chickens, milk, butter, cream and, soon after I turned ten, ice cream, for he had the courage to branch out and open an ice-cream stand. What better to do with the milk of fifty cows?

The fall also brought horror with the killing of the pig. Chickens at least provided some humour to a seven-year-old by running around like chickens with their heads cut off after their heads had been cut off. It sounds grotesque now, but my brother and I thought it wonderful, perhaps because it was such an upset of the normal.

But the pigs were different. Each year, he had a name, and we'd grow familiar with him by feeding him kitchen scraps, scratching behind his ears, laughing at the way he wallowed in the mud during the summer. So what we saw was shocking, and neither of us watched it after the first time. I still remember the blood. And thinking my grandfather was a monster, at least for a week.

The poor man suffered another week of monster-dom when we learned that the calves were sent to the slaughterhouse and not, as we'd decided must happen, off to grow up on other farms. The fate of the turkeys, chickens, pigs, and calves, it should be noted, in no way affected what my brother and I liked to eat. There was only one vegetarian in the family, my aunt by marriage, Jean, who was not only vegetarian, but politically to the left of everyone else in the family, probably to the left of everyone in the state of New Jersey. My grandfather called her 'The Agitator', but she seemed the person with whom he spent the most time in conversation and whose opinion he seemed most to value.

I remember the arrival of Sal, the blacksmith, who came by every two or three months to put new shoes on the horses. He drove a battered pickup truck and had somehow built a forge on the back of it. As soon as he parked his truck, he started a fire with wood, then gradually added coal to it. While it was growing smaller and hotter, the farmhands brought out what-ever horses happened to need new shoes, either the farm's horses or those stabled there by their suburban owners.

My brother and I were made to stand, always, at least a horse's leg away from the truck, in case one of them decided to try to kick her way out of her new shoes. This seldom happened: Sal's union with the horses seemed almost magical, a kind of interspecies ballet. He guided their legs and feet as though they were part of his own body, placed them between his leather-aproned knees and banged, pried, grated, cut, excavated, and filed until the horse's foot was freed of all dirt or nails and absolutely flat, any excess growth sliced away on all sides.

My memory has Sal pulling the fresh shoe from the fire with a pair of tongs, hammering it to perfect flatness, then thrusting it into a barrel of water to cool, but in recent years, when I've watched farriers work, I've seen no fire and have missed the frightening *hisssss* of the water as a piece of red-hot iron was plunged into it.

A few years ago, archaeologists in northern Britain discovered two pairs of 'hipposandals', metal slippers that were somehow attached to the feet of a horse, not nailed to them. Looking at the photo, I suspected they could just as easily be two sets of elaborate candleholders, but if the archaeologists want them to be horse slippers, I'll believe them. I like to think, my memory of Sal and the horses still so strong, that the same rapport existed between the animals and the men who tied on their fancy slippers.

Eventually, my grandfather had to give up the farm and sold it – curse the day – to a housing developer, who knocked down the stone farmhouse and the barns and built modern, not very interesting houses. In the centre of the field in front of the house, there stood, for centuries before my grandfather built the house, an enormous purple beech tree. For my brother and me, and for my twenty-nine cousins, the tree was a hiding place, a climbing place, a sitting and thinking place, and a meeting place. It survived the construction of the houses, lived on untouched until at least the 1970s, when I last passed by on my way to New York. I've not returned since then because I don't want it not to be there.

2. My Family

It's the opening line in *Anna Karenina*, isn't it, the one about happy families being the same and unhappy ones being unhappy in their own way? Because it's Tolstoy, and he presumably knew about such things, I'll let it pass, though it occurs to me that what families are in their own way is weird. Perhaps happy or unhappy, but decidedly weird. As kids, we assume that our family is the standard, for that's what we see. After all, we end up talking the way they do, having their social and fiscal ideas, dealing with stress or drink or the law in pretty much the same way they do, so it's but a little jump to thinking that such behaviour is normal, no matter how peculiar that behaviour might be.

We observe strangeness in other people and in their families. God knows, I saw a fair bit of it when I was a kid. But perhaps because we have so little experience of the world, we don't register it as weirdness at the time and don't come to that assessment until we're older. At the time, we're so busy learning and seeing and looking around that we have little time for judgement or discernment: we just take it in.

It is only later that we come to judge or at least take a critical stance, or maybe what we do is turn an objective eye on what appeared normal and, in the process, see that it might not have been so.

In this context, I think of Dickens and all those bizarre minor characters who fill his books: the old man who tosses sofa cushions at his wife to get her attention; Wemmick and his aged parent; Uriah Heep. When we first read these books, the characters seem unreal, almost as though they've been dropped down from another planet. It is not until we reread the books as adults that we realize how filled the world is with Uriah Heeps and how much soft aggression exists in many marriages. So when we look back on our families from the vantage point of adulthood, perhaps of age, we begin to see that some of the things they did might have been more than a little strange.

Part of the cast during my childhood were my mother's three aunts, who lived together in a twelve-room house not far from the farm. Aunt Trace was a widow, though I never learned more about her husband than that he had been a pharmacist (this created endless room for speculation as to the cause of his death); Aunt Gert and Aunt Mad had never married. These three women lived in perfect harmony in the house, and by the time I was old enough to visit them they no longer worked, if, in fact, they ever had.

They played cards, specifically bridge. Their days were filled with cards, as were their evenings. They had a circle of women friends with whom they played. Because they went to church on Sunday, they did not play bridge on Sunday, not unless the church had a bridge evening. And Gert cheated. My mother delighted in telling me about this, since Gert was a pillar of the church. Over the years, she had developed a language of dithering and hesitation that was as clear a signal to her partner as if she had laid her cards face up on the table. 'Oh, I think I'll just risk one heart.' 'I wonder if I dare raise that bid to two clubs?' Since I never played bridge, I can't decode these messages; it was enough for us to know she cheated. The stakes were perhaps, after four hours of play, a dollar. But she cheated. She also gave thousands of dollars to charity every year and was wonderfully generous with every member of a large, and generally thankless, family, but cheat she would.

Gert also had a 'colored' friend, quite a rarity in New Jersey in the 1950s, who was part of her bridge circle. None of the other women wanted her as their partner, so Gert always chose her. The woman played badly and so Gert would always lose when they played together, but bring her she would and play with her she did. And invite her to Christmas dinner, by God.

I remember little things about Gert. She always put the flowers in the refrigerator at night so they would last longer; she telephoned and complained to the parents of any child who stepped on her grass; she always wore a hat when leaving the house. Towards the end of her life, after Mad and Trace had died, she was left alone in the twelve-room house and was eventually persuaded to sell it and move to a mere six rooms. She died soon thereafter and left, in the linen closet, the sheets and towels that had been part of her dowry. Beautiful, hand-embroidered linen and all unused. I still have six table napkins.

Uncle Joe the plumber was another member of the family. All Joe ever wanted to be was a farmer, but his father insisted that he learn a trade, and so Joe became a plumber, and a good one, though I know he didn't much like being a plumber. The only thing he had to say on the subject, when I asked him what he had to know to be a plumber, was, 'Payday's Friday and shit don't flow uphill.' In his middle years, he moved away from the city to a farm in northern New Jersey, where he abandoned pipes and sinks and rode his tractor all day, planting and harvesting and happy as a mudlark. In front of his house he built a small wooden stand, where he sold fresh flowers and vegetables. He spent his evenings poring over seed catalogues and, it would appear, his investment folder, for he died a multimillionaire.

My brother, three years older than I, also inherited my mother's general chipper stance towards the world, as well as the almost total lack of ambition that has characterized our lives. And he has, to a remarkable degree, what the Italians would call the ability to *arrangiarsi*, to find a solution, to find a way to get around a problem, land on his feet.

Nowhere is this better illustrated than in the story of the dirt. His last job, before he retired, was as manager of an apartment complex of about a hundred apartments. His job was to administer contracts and rent payments and to see that the buildings were sufficiently well cared for. At a certain point, the owners decided to convert the buildings to gas heat, and that meant the old oil-burning system had to be removed, as well as the storage tank that lay under one of the parking lots.

The demolition men came and took out the furnace, then dug up the tank and removed it. Whereupon arrived the inspectors from the Environmental Protection Agency, declaring that, because the tank had sprung a leak sometime in the past and spilled oil into the earth, the dirt that had been piled up around it was both contaminated and sequestered and could not be removed save by paying a special haulage company to come and take it away.

My brother, long a resident of the town, knew a bit more than the average citizen about the connection between the inspectors and the haulage company because of his hunting buddies, some of whom belonged to an organization that – hmm, how to express this delicately – worked at some variance to the law. (We're in New Jersey, Italians, the building trade … get it?) And so he had some suspicions about the actual level of contamination in the dirt.

As fortune would have it, he was about to leave for two weeks of vacation, and so, the night before he left, he called one of his hunting pals, who just happened to be in the business of supplying landfill to various building projects and just happened to be a member of that same organization. My brother explained that he was going to be away for some time and that his friend, whose name he never disclosed to me, was free to come in at any time during the next two weeks and pick up the dirt that surrounded the excavated hole where the tank had been. The only caveat was that the trucks had to be unmarked and had to come at night.

Two weeks later, tanned and fit, he and his wife returned from vacation, and as he stepped out of the taxi that had brought them from the airport, he looked about, like a good custodian, at the buildings and grounds that were in his care. Shocked by what he saw, he slapped his hand to his forehead and exclaimed, 'My God, they've stolen my dirt,' whereupon he went inside and called the police to report the theft.

The same was to be found on my father's side of the family, though legend rather than witnesses provides the suggestion of strangeness. There was his uncle Raoul, bilingual in Spanish and English, who always answered the phone in heavily accented English and, when he found himself asked for, responded that he was the butler but would go and enquire 'if Meester Leon was libre'. It was Raoul, as well, who once got in a taxi in front of his New York hotel and had himself taken to Boston.

My father's uncle Bill lived in a vast, sprawling mansion about fifty miles north of New York City and often disappeared for short or long periods of time to the various banana republics of South and Central America. The official story was that he was in the coffee trade, but then why all those other stories about meeting various heads of state while surrounded by machine-gun-toting guards?

Uncle Bill was married to the painted woman of the family, Aunt Florence, who suffered the dual handicap of being not only divorced but Jewish, married into a Spanish-Irish Catholic family. Further, they had lived together 'in sin', as one said then, before their union was sanctioned by the state, the clergy wanting no part of them. In the face of these impediments, we were all more than willing to overlook the fact that she bore a frightening resemblance to a horse and was, to boot, significantly less intelligent than one. Her mantra, which she repeated openly whenever we visited, was that a woman must pretend to be stupid so that a man would marry her. My brother and I never saw evidence that she was pretending.

And yes, this comes to me now that I think about them: Henry. Henry was their Japanese cook, a sort of unseen presence who was said to be in the kitchen, though none of us ever laid eyes on him. It is part of family lore that Henry wrote in his will that he left his life savings to the United States. Because no will was found when he died and there was no living relative, he got his wish.

My father's brother, my uncle, a man of stunning handsomeness in the photos we still have of him, was an officer in the merchant marine. He was rumoured, though neither my brother nor I can recall the source of this rumour, to have been a lover of Isadora Duncan, though surely I was too young to know who she was when I first heard this story.

Family memories, family mysteries.

3. Halloween

It is only to other Americans that I dare say that my mother was a lunatic, for only they have heard, over the years, how the word has softened and no longer refers to a mad person screaming that the Day of Judgement is at hand. Instead, it can mean, and often does, a person with an unusual sense of humour or a taste for the absurd. It is in this way that I use it when speaking of my mother, a woman who looked at the world, as Emily Dickinson said, 'slant'.

My first memories of her have her laughing, taking us to her father's farm, where my brother and I would be held up to look the cows in the eye or even sit on the backs of the giant draught horses, who seemed to us as big as houses. She's the one who led us up the ladder in the barn and taught us how to launch ourselves from the upper level onto the hay-filled wagons. Every few months, she'd arrive at our school an hour before it was time to go home and tell the principal that we had to go and visit an aunt in the hospital, or the dentist, or the doctor, and she'd take us to the farm to let us watch Sal the black-smith shoe the horses or fix a piece of farm machinery by welding two pieces of metal together. I fear she thus instilled in us the elastic vision we both have of the truth.

Another quality she passed on to us was her restless energy, for she was a woman who loved to do things, to make things: she taught herself how to replace the caning on chairs, to refinish furniture, to hang wall-paper, to replace a pane of glass, and countless other things I wish I'd learned to do. She was a dreadful cook, save for sweets and cakes, but we were kids and so didn't notice. My father, he too a man of good spirit, forbore and ate a lot of peanuts.

Halloween is a typically American holiday: people pretend to be what they are not in hopes of reward. In my childhood, it took the form of our going door to door, badly disguised or costumed, in the hope that people would answer the door and give us candy. My mother, unlike most parents of her generation, consid-ered it rather stupid for children to roam around the neighbourhood, most of them wrapped in old sheets and pretending to be ghosts, going from door to door, begging. She was bored with the soldiers, pilots, pirates, nurses, and policemen who came to our door and equally tired of her own children's lack of imagin-ation in choosing what to pretend to be.

Our family also included a dog, Sooner, a smooth-haired beige dog of uncertain pedigree about the size of an Irish terrier, though she was neither Irish nor a terrier. She was simply a happy dog who was in love with my mother and tolerated the rest of us, perhaps even liked us.

One year – I must have been ten – a few days before Halloween, my mother asked us what we wanted to be. Unwilling to suggest 'ghost', I tried out 'spaceman', a word that jumped from my mouth before I'd given it any thought. My brother said he'd be a cowboy, and my mother moaned.

She lit a cigarette (people smoked then, everywhere, all the time; she died at eighty-four and swam laps in the local swimming pool until she was eighty-two) and looked from me to my brother and back at me, perhaps wondering how these conventional, uninteresting creatures could possibly have gotten there, could possibly be *hers*.

Before she could say anything, Sooner slipped out from her place under my mother's chair, stood on her back legs, and put one paw in my mother's lap. She made a small, doggy noise.

'You what?' my mother asked her in a conversational tone.

Sooner made another noise.

'A lion?' my mother asked. She took a long drag on her cigarette, studied the curtains, exhaled slowly, looked carefully at Sooner, looked at me and my brother, stubbed out her cigarette, and said, 'Why not?'

And that began it. Each year, from then on, Sooner went out begging, with us and for us, at Halloween, and because we'd contributed to her costume, we got to keep the candy and apples and whatever else she was given. We were also spared what we now viewed as the nonsense of putting on a costume.

The first year was the lion year. Lions have manes; my mother's maiden aunt Gert's prize sartorial possession was a single fox fur meant to be wrapped around the neck and fixed, head hanging down in front, tail hanging next to it. To get this from Aunt Gert required the invention of a wedding my mother had to attend, looking her best by wearing the fur.

Aunt Gert fell for it like a ripe plum. The rest of the lion's fur was easy: Sooner was beige. But lions have claws and very large feet. Four grey pot holders with just the tips of knitting needles sticking out from the front supplied the paws; the tail was a piece of curtain cord with a pompom at the end.

From the following years, I remember a zebra, an elephant that required the cardboard tubes from four rolls of kitchen paper, and an utterly unconvincing polar bear made from the white pyjama suit of a cousin's three-month-old baby. (The trouble with many animals is that they have round heads. Dogs do not, nor do they like wearing anything over their heads.) Thus the polar bear had an elongated head and snout. Beige.

The last year we did it, my mother went all out and transformed Sooner into a cheerleader. She spent October knitting a white woollen football sweater with four very short sleeves in a size with a minus sign before it, the number 28 in red on the back. The short skirt was again Aunt Gert's gift: an ancient silk brocade lampshade, tassels at the bottom and, luckily, the proper size to be slipped around Sooner's waist, an anatomical part not common to dogs. Perhaps sensing that this was the last year we'd bother with such

childish things, Sooner finally permitted her head to
be utilized and wore a wig, for the construction of
which my mother sacrificed her rubber swimming cap
and spent considerable time punching holes in the
rubber and pulling through single strands of yellow
knitting wool. To her chagrin, she failed to invent two
pairs of sneakers, so Sooner wore her own feet. If nothing else, this did make it easier for her to walk with us
from house to house as we shouted 'Trick or treat' and
waited for the doors to open.

4. First Day of School

So traumatic was my introduction to school that I marvel I remained there so many years. School started when kids were six. Off we went to kindergarten, there to be taught the rudiments of civilization – the letters of the alphabet, the names of animals, fruits, workers, colors, shapes. There were some complex skills: sitting still when told to do so, working at a task until it was completed, not snatching objects from other kids, asking permission to do what we wanted to do.

That, however, came after school began. First I had to get there. In early September, there had been, of course, Signs and Portents that change was coming: a new dress and lovely little black shoes, my very first pair of black Mary Janes, with a buckle that took forever to close. And a lunch box: metal, with Donald Duck on the cover, and inside it a thermos bottle for milk and space for a sandwich and a banana. I had managed to avoid wondering what all these new things were for. My brother had had three first days of school so far, and thus I'd come to associate it with new things and a sense of beginning all over again. If he got new things, then why shouldn't I?

I was not told any more than that I was going along to school with my big brother, Albert. Nothing was said about staying, and I suppose I didn't want to understand the significance of my now full lunch box: perhaps it would be necessary for my mother and me to stop and have something to eat before we drove back home, my mother and I, together?

I sat in my regular seat, behind my mother; my brother always got to sit in front. I knew the way because I'd gone along those few times he'd missed the school bus and had to be driven there. I watched the houses pass us by, knew we had to stop when the light turned red, up and across the overpass of the highway that led to New York, right at the corner and down to the end of the street.

There were lots of mothers, lots of kids and cars and the school bus pulling up. My brother got out, eager to see all of his friends again. My mother got out and opened my door, saying we'd go and say hello. This made no sense to me, because if we said anything to my brother, it should be goodbye before we went home. I remember that my mother reached into the back seat and picked up my new lunch box.

We walked around the car and my mother called to my brother, who came over. Stooping down, she said, 'You get to go to school today, too, Donna.' She smiled and handed me the lunch box and I, stunned, took it.

She stood and I began to whimper. She took a step towards the car, and I started to cry. She put her hand on the door, and I began to scream. My brother wrapped his arms around me and held me tight while the car drove away, down to the beginning of the street and left, and then it was gone, and I realized I didn't know the way home.

5. Reading

I come, luckily, from a family of readers. My parents were readers; thus I grew up with the example of adults who sat for hours, reading books. They read not only for themselves, but to me and my brother, so some of my earliest memories are of *The Three Billy Goats Gruff*, *Little Red Riding Hood*, and a book about a choo-choo train whose name eludes me. My immediate interest was, of course, in the pictures, but there came a time when the words and the stories became more appealing, though I'm not sure I remember just why that happened.

I still remember a book with word puzzles in it, and I remember the most enchanting of them. In English, 'wool' – indeed, any rough cloth surface – can be said to be fuzzy, fuzz being those little tufts of cloth or fibre that accumulate on sweaters and blankets after long use. Because kids love rhymes, especially silly ones, 'wuzzy' is often added to fuzzy to create 'fuzzy wuzzy', a perfect description of the fur of a teddy bear. Now, imagine a teddy bear whose name is Fuzzy Wuzzy but who, because he has been handled and loved for years, has had his fur rubbed, stroked, chewed, and worn away until he is entirely bald and smooth. And then this, which I still remember my mother reading to me:

> *Fuzzy Wuzzy was a bear.*
> *Fuzzy Wuzzy had no hair.*
> *Fuzzy Wuzzy wasn't fuzzy,*
> *Wuzzy?*

And I still remember the bolt of delight I felt as I grasped this miraculous truth: a word could have two separate meanings. Suddenly, language was revealed to me as the best toy, ever. Bicycles could go only one way: forward. Balls always rolled down the hill. The wind-up toy always ran down and stopped moving. But here was a source of infinite possibility, perhaps even a manifestation of perpetual motion, for one could, with sufficient cleverness, keep fooling around with words and make them mean different things, and just think of how many more words there were than, say, toys or bicycles.

Once I began to read on my own, I saw that language was also the source of tricks. There is the verbal riddle (which can't be kept secret if written because it is based on that terrible peculiarity of English: pronunciation that is entirely whimsical and answers to no rules or laws).

What's black and white and read all over?

When this is pronounced in English – and this is always a spoken riddle – the word 'read', because of its proximity to 'black' and 'white', and because it is pronounced the same way as 'red', will always be mistaken for the name of the color, rather than the past tense of the verb 'to read'. Native speakers are tricked by it; foreigners are mowed down by it.

Thus, while still a child I had examples of the miraculous deceitfulness of written words that confuse with their sound and spoken words that seem to have the right to mean whatever they please. Because I am a native English speaker, this untrustworthiness is a source of delight, not frustration. Further, it seems to me that English, and the English, are much given to this sort of verbal nonsense.

So here I am, many decades after taking delight in the ambiguity of Fuzzy Wuzzy, making my living by playing with words. It would be an exaggeration to suggest that Fuzzy Wuzzy set me on my life's path, but it is true to say that he was there – hairless – when I took the first step.

6. Tomato Empire

Americans of my generation sucked in the Protestant work ethic with our mother's milk. Like it or not, the idea that one was meant to study and work was one of the building blocks of our minds. Most of us had as little choice about going to university as we did about going to elementary school: that was what one did, and then one sailed off and got a job. Those of us who enjoyed studying simply stayed on board a little longer and let the ship carry us on to our doctoral studies, waving to our classmates as they rowed away to jobs as teachers or lawyers or engineers.

A person could pass years, decades, in graduate school: apply for another grant, accept a job as a professor's assistant. And the cruise went on.

At a certain point, however, the economic consequences of our absence from the real job market became evident. Fellowships and teaching assistantships allowed for genteel poverty, granola, and Birkenstocks, but they did not permit trips to the opera, much less to Italy.

The problem was best stated by Dickens, who has Wilkins Micawber opine that when inflow exceeds outflow, the result is happiness; when outflow exceeds inflow, the result is misery. Thus, it sometimes behoved me during the far too many years I remained in graduate school to ensure that inflow exceeded outflow, thereby sparing myself the misery of a year in which I did not spend a few months in Italy.

In the seventies, I lived in Amherst, Massachusetts, completing my studies at the university. My parents lived in New Jersey, only a few hours away. I visited them occasionally. My mother, a passionate gardener, always planted a few dozen tomato plants; I have no idea why, since it is impossible for two people to consume the produce of more than a few. The garden was at the back of the property but was distantly visible from the major road on which our house was located.

Newton's apple fell one afternoon when I was visiting, working in the garden with my mother. A woman approached and asked if she could buy some of my mother's tomatoes. Nothing better than home-grown, is there? My mother refused, filled the woman's arms with tomatoes, and sent her away happy. Then, turning to me, my mother said, laughing, 'I could probably make a fortune if I sold them instead of giving them away.'

Sold them instead of giving them away? Sold them instead of giving them away? Sold them instead of giving them away? Could Karl Marx have asked a better question?

It was then legal, in the state of New Jersey, to sell produce from your garden, so long as you both grew and sold it on your own land. A few miles from my parents' home, an old friend of theirs had a commercial farm, where the public could go and pick tomatoes or peaches and then pay by the basket. Is not the key to commercial enterprise the difference between wholesale and retail prices?

The next morning, I arrived at Mr Vreeland's farm at seven and picked and paid for six or seven large baskets of tomatoes and took them back to my parents' home. I grabbed a collapsible table, covered it with an old oilcloth, and placed upon it a few small wicker baskets, each containing about a kilo of tomatoes. I set it up at the side of the road and turned my attention to the reading I had to prepare for the coming semester: if memory serves, *Sir Gawain and the Green Knight* and *Beowulf.*

By two that afternoon, Grendel and his mother were dead and I'd read and taken notes on the first pages of *Gawain.* And sold all of the tomatoes. The next morning, I doubled the number of baskets I filled, which meant – ah, capitalism flows like ichor in our veins – I doubled my earnings.

This was August and I still had three weeks of the summer break before I had to resume teaching at the university. My parents were happy to have me extend my visit, I had my books, and so why not?

The rhythm was an easy one to fall into: at dawn I was in the fields, where I worked for an hour or two, swatting mosquitoes the size of bumblebees and surprising the odd field mouse, but always increasing the number of baskets until the back of my Volkswagen Beetle sank down on its axle under their weight.

By this time, word had spread about the tomato stand and I'd already acquired some regular customers. Some asked if the tomatoes were grown in my own garden and I would self-righteously point back to my mother's garden, where the plants thrived and could be seen to be doing so. Others asked if I used pesticides and I would give a scandalized, 'Certainly not,' though God alone knew what Mr Vreeland poured, pumped, or sprayed upon them when no one was around to see.

Occasionally, when I got bored with it, I'd leave a cup on the table for a few hours and ask people to help themselves and leave their money. Very few people took the opportunity to steal, though most of them did switch the tomatoes in the boxes to suit their taste in size and ripeness.

And then came Harry. My best friend and her husband, who lived in New York, had recently gotten a Scottish terrier puppy, Harry, who was in the ball of fluff stage of his development. But then they decided to go on vacation, and where oh where could they leave Harry? Thus Harry joined the firm, sleeping or rolling around with his tennis ball under the table, occasionally following customers to their cars and trying to jump in with them, never lifting a paw to help with either picking or packaging, but still a great public relations asset to the corporation. Soon I repeatedly had to make it clear that though the tomatoes were for sale, Harry was not. He kept me company for two weeks, always cheerful, always ready to chase a ball or have his stomach scratched: of how many employees can that be said? Though he was happy to see his owners when they came to pick him up, I like to think he regretted the separation.

University classes resumed and I returned to Massachusetts. Perhaps it was the sight of my fellowship contract and that distressingly low sum I was to be paid that had me back in New Jersey on the second weekend of classes, returning to my tomato empire and earning on a weekend what the university paid me in a month. Or perhaps it was nothing more than my heritage, the Protestant work ethic.

7. Christmas Turkey

Many of the people I've met in the world of food insist that most cooks are either food cooks or cake cooks. If this is true, then my mother was definitely a cake cook: to her, dinner was what one ate on the way to dessert, and who can find fault in this? Give that woman a cup of sugar, a pound of butter, a dozen eggs, and a bag of flour and she became to cake what Stradivarius was to the violin. Cakes and cookies, brownies and puddings, pies and muffins flew out of her kitchen on angel wings. Christmas threw her into an orgy of cookie-making, though any day of the year was cause for Key lime pie or fudge.

She ate like a trooper and remained rail-thin all her life, no doubt because she smoked like a Turk. There should be a monument to her in Cuba, or wherever sugar is grown today, and she would have made fast work of the European butter mountain. Why my brother and I were not child diabetics is one of the great mysteries of medical science.

Ah, but let me return my thoughts to the food, the real food. A few classic recipes in her repertoire were spaghetti sauce (canned tomatoes, no garlic), fried ham steaks, and baked beans. The beans, I recall, started life in the can, which reminds me that it was not until I was living in Italy that I discovered that mayonnaise does not live in a container but can be made from egg yolks and olive oil. But my mother's supreme culinary triumph, which has remained in the memory of all who knew her, was the Christmas turkey.

American turkeys resemble Americans in that they are significantly larger than turkeys found in other parts of the world – and those chosen to feed a family of four can be as large as ten kilos. Further, they had and still have an inordinate amount of breast, having been bred to answer the American preference for white meat. There are stories – one reads them in all the anti-globalization magazines – about the chickens who fall forward on to their beaks from the weight of their overbred breasts. So too these poor turkeys.

Because of their size, they demanded a large oven and an enormous roasting pan, and had to be cooked for a very long time. And thus the Christmas culinary ritual as it evolved in our family.

My mother had either acquired or inherited the notion that turkey had to be well done. Now, 'well done' is a concept open to interpretation and variation, is it not? Does 'well done' mean that blood can no longer be seen when the turkey is carved? Does it mean that the skin on the breast is crisp and dark brown? Or does it mean something more sinister?

There is a legend in the family that one of the ancestors of my mother's father was at least part Native
American, and it is only to this that I am able to attrib-
ute my mother's interest in pemmican, that dried meat
which Native Americans are said to have carried with
them on long journeys. Thin strips of – I believe – buf-
falo were suspended over open fires and slowly
smoked until they were free of all moisture and could
thus endure without spoiling for months, perhaps
years.

No, my mother did not wear a feather headdress
while cooking the Christmas turkey, but she was
clearly bent on turning it into pemmican. We had a gas
oven as opposed to an open fire, but that did not deter
her for an instant in her efforts: the bird was to be
reduced to dried meat.

This meant that those of us who were aware of the
atavistic urge of her ancestry would, during the endless hours in which the beast was being transformed
into powder in the oven, see to it that my mother's
glass of Christmas punch was kept full and that she
was kept busy in conversation in the living room. Each
time she said something about going out to the kitchen
to 'check on the turkey', one of us would jump up and
say, 'Oh, I was just going out to get a carrot, so I'll have
a look,' or, 'Maybe I'll go stir the onions and see how
it's doing.'

Whoever went out to the kitchen would turn down
the oven, set by my mother to a temperature just below
that required to forge steel; the bolder ones turned it
off. Soon the urge to check on the turkey would sweep
over her, to be kept at bay only by refilling her
punch glass or offering her a cigarette. A friend once

introduced the brilliant variation of, 'Oh, just sit there and have another sip of punch – nothing's going to happen to that poor turkey if you do,' which instantly became a Christmas standard.

Sooner or later, of course, she would make it to the kitchen and discover the lower temperature or the cooling oven. But by then she had had sufficient punch, so was inclined to blame it on her own forgetfulness, an opinion in which we all, quite mercilessly, joined her.

Finally, however, she would determine – by signs visible only to her and perhaps her Native American ancestors – that the turkey was cooked and it was time to eat, and so we gathered around the table for the regular Christmas dinner: turkey/pemmican, onion and apple dressing, creamed parsnips, cranberry sauce, peas, and mashed potatoes. (The secret of this recipe is to add *equal amounts* of potato and butter. This cannot fail.)

Invariably, after grace (certainly the most embarrassing moment of the year for all of us, regardless of age or religious affiliation) we waited as my father carved the turkey, considerably reduced in size as a result of its long stay in the oven. And then we ate as much of it as we could.

The napkins were the linen ones inherited from my Irish grandmother, so no one dared hide the turkey there, though my aunt Jean, of happy memory, would eat Christmas dinner with her purse on her lap, opening it repeatedly. My uncle Joe always brought his hunting dog, and it sat by his side for the entire meal.

Though great inroads were made into the turkey, large portions of it always remained, only to be transformed, during the week that followed, into turkey in gravy, turkey hash, and turkey sandwiches. Its disappearance was usually linked to that of the Christmas tree, though sometimes, in the form of soup, it survived even the tree.

8. *Tosca*

All right, I confess. I tell you, I confess. Stop hitting me on the head with the phone book; stop shining those bright lights into my eyes. I confess, I confess. Stop putting those bamboo sticks under my fingernails. You don't have to do that. I confess. I told you. I LOVE *TOSCA*.

All right. Do you want me to say it again? (Thank you for turning off the light. Now put down the phone book, please.) I LOVE *TOSCA*.

There, I've said it. Write it out and I'll sign it. I don't care that my confession will ruin my reputation, make me a laughing stock for being attracted to such a ... well, what is it that the American music critic Joseph Kerman called it, 'that shabby little shocker'? Hmm, not a nice thing to say about the opera, is it, however true it might be. But write it out anyway, and I'll sign it.

What's that, Officer? You want to know how it happened? Are you sure? OK, you pull out the bamboo
sticks, and I'll tell you.

Oh, that feels so much better, Officer. Thank you so
much.

All right, here's how it happened. It must have
been in the early sixties, when I was working in
New York. I'd always liked classical music but had
never listened to opera except once in a while on the
radio, the Saturday matinee from the Metropolitan
Opera.

Out of nothing but curiosity, I decided I might as
well go to the opera. Lots of people liked it, didn't
they? And since one was the same as every other, I
chose *Tosca*, having no idea at all of what it was
about.

The only ticket I could get at the old Metropolitan
Opera was for a standing-room place in the Family
Circle, just under the roof. I got there with enough time
to read the story, which sounded a bit tempestuous,
but this was opera, after all.

So there I stood, in the midst of a number of people
who gave the distinct impression that they seldom
left their apartments in daylight. They all spoke
knowingly about the production, the singers, the conductor, all of them impassioned in their defence of
their opinions.

The lights went down, everyone grew silent, the
curtain rose – hoo ha! I was going to the opera for the
first time. We were in church, and there was a handsome guy – not that this was discernible from the
Family Circle – apparently painting a woman's

portrait, which seemed a strange thing to be doing in a church. But this was opera, so who knew?

There was a bit of cheerful music and a bit of scuttling around, and then from offstage a female voice sang out, 'Mario! Mario! Mario!' and a woman not at all appropriately dressed for churchgoing, and carrying a bouquet of flowers the size of a Newfoundland, swept onstage.

This was Zinka Milanov, a name with which I was entirely unfamiliar, as I had been with *Tosca*. If lightning had struck me – unlikely, given the fact that I was indoors – I could not have been more stunned. I stood motionless until the end of the first act. I'd read the story, so I knew who they were: she the diva, he the painter, Scarpia the super-bad guy. The story was easy to follow, and I understood the passion, and then – ZOWIE! – that final Te Deum, with about 712 people on the stage.

I think I did not breathe during the intermission, afraid that I'd break something if I did. The second act: false politeness, violence, torture, sexual blackmail, *'Vissi d'arte'*, which even a philistine such as I could tell was glorious, and then murder. And then – my heart still pounds when I think about it – she stood over the corpse of the man she'd killed and all but whispered, *'E davanti a lui tremava tutta Roma!'* before, hands still red with Scarpia's blood, slipping out of the room to go and save her lover.

During the second intermission I had to sit down. People had left (how was this possible?), so there were empty seats, in one of which I put myself and sat for twenty minutes, listening to my heart beat.

I knew what was going to happen, and as the third act began I wanted to warn them that it was a set-up and they were both doomed. Somehow, any way, I wanted to enter into this artistic reality and change things, give them a happy ending. But I knew.

So the charade played its way to the end: poor Cavaradossi got to sing his heart out in his one full aria and then to play the hero, thinking the bullets would be fake, and poor Floria applauded him as he fell, an artist who knew how to play a death scene. And those of us who knew stood or sat there, made of stone, terrified of what was really going to happen, transported to some other place by the beauty with which it was happening.

'*Presto! Su, Andiamo!*' she called as she bent over him, and then those same words as at the opening, 'Mario! Mario!', but, oh, we'd come a long hard way to get to hear them again. The world's been turned upside down and evil has triumphed, and all is lost and soon Tosca will be lost, too, poor dear. All she wanted to do was live for art and love. She never hurt anyone, helped the poor, gave jewels to the Madonna, and God repays her like this.

And then she jumped. Those three hours changed my life. That sounds melodramatic, I know, but they did. I was hooked and went often, saw in the next twenty years the great singers of my time: Scotto, Pavarotti, Caballé, Domingo, Price, Sills, Olivero. (Yes, Magda Olivero – I saw her debut at the Met at the age of sixty-five. In *Tosca*.) Nilsson, Di Stefano, del Monaco, Corelli, Gobbi, Christoff.

In a way, these years ruined me, for I am now one of those old farts who, upon hearing the great singers of the present age, murmurs polite things about them and says, 'Yes, yes, yes,' and remember how spines shook when Nilsson sang Turandot and the heavens opened when Leontyne Price sang spirituals.

Or when Zinka Milanov sang Tosca.

9. Handel

Jesus might not be my Personal Saviour, but the *Messiah* blessed my life. I heard it first, probably at some Christmas concert, when I was in high school, performed the way it was in the sixties: with an orchestra of hundreds, or so it seemed, and an even larger chorus. Exposed to my first experience of baroque vocal music, I thought the earth had dropped out from beneath my chair or I had been launched into space, for this was a new musical world.

Who knows why I had started listening to classical music as a teenager, when my friends were mad for Peggy Lee and Elvis. My family certainly wasn't musical, and none of my friends were drawn to classical music: I simply liked the sound of it. I stumbled along, listening to it on the radio, then buying records, passing through a trajectory that appears to have been common to others of my age: Ravel, Tchaikovsky,

Grieg, Rimsky-Korsakov, the Brahms symphonies. And the music I listened to, I *liked*! I'm sure I'd find it less embarrassing today to confess to having used drugs, had I done so.

With the greater autonomy presented by university life, I started attending concerts and broadened my taste, but it was always a hit or miss thing, and I never, then or now, learned how to read musical notation. I liked what I heard: it's as simple as that. Because classical music was then played on many radio stations, it was possible to discover a new piece, like it, then go and find a recording and hear it again.

Opera came crashing into my life while I was working at my first job in New York, those first hours in the standing-room section of the Old Met in the early sixties, watching and hearing my first opera: *Tosca*, with Zinka Milanov, no longer even in the third flush of her youth, singing of pain and loss. And I, like Tosca, was lost. This was a second new world, one that added drama to the music, then tossed in the glory of the human voice.

At the same time that I was discovering the vocal glories of Donizetti and Verdi and Rossini and Puccini, my symphonic ear remained attuned to Handel, not because I didn't like his vocal music but because, aside from *Messiah*, there simply was nothing else on offer: the dramatic oratorios and the operas were almost never performed, and surely never in the major theatres. But then – I believe it was in 1965 – the New York City Opera took a chance with *Giulio Cesare*, with Beverly Sills singing Cleopatra, and those performances introduced New York to baroque opera.

Listening to the recording of it today, after several decades, it sounds dated and 'wrong' – whatever that means – in comparison to the way the music is performed now. But the magic is there, and we are all heirs of that production.

At the same time that I can write of 'magic' and how music provides me with pleasure beyond measure, I must also confess that I'm sick of music. I'm sick of hearing it everywhere: while I wait to speak to the electric company, while I wait for a train or a plane, or stand in line in a post office, or while I'm having dinner in a restaurant. (Sartre got it wrong, by the way: hell is not other people. Hell is *The Four Seasons*.) Like air pollution, it is everywhere. And it pollutes.

Aside from those times when I choose to listen attentively to a particular recording or attend a live performance, I listen to music less and less, perhaps because I want, at least in my own life, to prevent it from becoming wallpaper. I want to listen to music, to tune into the living current that exists between the musician and the audience. I do not want to hear music as the background to a conversation, just as I do not want to have a conversation during a performance of *Coriolanus*. I do not go to the opera to talk, and I do not read a book while listening to *Semiramide*: fusion is bad enough in food.

But this is to preach, and I would rather hope. I hope that people raised in a world where classical music is watered down to near banality by its very surfeit in inappropriate places will sometime experience it alone and find in it the comfort and exaltation of spirit that

Beauty can bring. Further, I hope it will thrill and upset them, leave them feeling weak.

It's not going to change the world, music isn't, nor will listening to it; it hasn't managed to do so since our ancestors squatted around fires, chanting. It can, however, change the individual life by enhancing both the consciousness and the imagination of the listener. It seems to me that these are mighty things.

10. Moo

She was a woman who loved a cigarette and a drink. Now, I realize this is hardly the way to begin an article that will probably end up being a hymn to my mommy, but it is what comes to mind when those of us who loved her talk about her or think of her. She smoked from the time she was sixteen, a pack a day, and she smoked until a few years before her death, when, from one day to the next, she stopped, almost as if she'd suddenly forgotten that cigarettes existed. As for the drink, remember that she was a woman of her time, born in 1916, and so she had no truck with wine drinking or Prosecco or Bellinis. The woman liked a drink: a gin and tonic, a martini (the recipe for which was to put some gin in a shaker of ice with a bit of lemon peel, shake the hell out of it, then whisper 'vermouth' before pouring it into a glass), or a daiquiri. She had one before dinner, and she did this until about the time she gave up on cigarettes.

She was a farm girl, my mother was, the middle of the nine children born to Joseph A. Noll, dairy farmer, born in Nuremberg, who emigrated to New Jersey when he was eighteen, and Jennie Mullins, born soon after her own parents emigrated from Ireland. They gave my mother the name of Mildred, which she never liked; by the time I came along, one of my many cousins had renamed her Aunt Moo, and so Moo she became, and remained, to everyone except me and my brother, who called her 'Ma'. She grew up on the farm, doing all those things that people thirty miles from New York City no longer know about: milking cows, watching chickens run around after their heads are cut off, making the trip into New York with my grandfather every month, two days after payday, to collect the Irish farmhands.

The process of memory is odd, isn't it? Do we remember things because we were there and saw them, or because we've been told them so often that they've been forced to become real? I remember a dog we had, Grumpy, a springer spaniel, stubborn as a mule and stupid with it, who refused to be left alone in the house. Family legend has it that he once broke through the bottom window of the glass door to the veranda, then later chewed through the leg of the chair wedged in front of the window to break through it again. I had a photo of my mother holding Grumpy, lost in one of the many moves I've made.

If one of my mother's hands was usually busy with a cigarette, the other often held the telephone. She became, as years passed and her siblings married and moved off here and there, the central information office of the family. So she'd be the first to know that Vern's husband had lost his job again or that Howard was in the hospital. Only later did I learn that she was also the keeper of the family secrets. She was the one who could be told the bad things: the violent husband, the rent not paid, the drinking. Her sisters often came to visit, and endless confidences were exchanged at the kitchen table while my cousins and I were sent out to play.

I was never told what was discussed in those long, sometimes tearful conversations, and it was only by osmosis, I guess, that she taught me that what was told in confidence could never be repeated. Not 'should never', but 'could never'.

Then there were the gardens, which she created anywhere we lived. My father would be enlisted to do the original heavy digging, but then it was hers. Flowers: she wanted to see an ocean of flowers from every window of every house we ever lived in, and she managed it. I can still see her, kneeling in the dirt, filthy to her elbows, yanking at weeds or digging a hole to slip in a tiny flower plant, relentless, the design of the garden clear in her imagination. The house held vases of flowers from spring until fall, either hers or flowers given to her by her garden pals.

Perhaps because she was born during one war and lived through another, she loved a bargain. Even better, she loved to get something for free, especially plants. She once learned that the farm of a friend of her father's had been sold and was going to be asphalted over and turned into a shopping centre. I still remember our midnight mission, a week before the project began, to go and dig up the white violets that grew on the farm's manure pile. I'd signed on for the violets. But when they were stashed on the back seat of the car, she opened the trunk and pulled out a stack of baskets, telling me we were going to take the manure pile as well. When I attempted to protest, her indignant 'But this is *horse* manure!' silenced me instantly.

I don't know much about genes or their structure, but I do know that children often resemble their parents in spirit. Depression runs in families, does it not? So then why not happiness? My mother was a happy person, and my brother and I tend towards cheerfulness, always have. My father was generally well disposed towards the world, but she managed to find an endless number of things that made her happy.

She was a reader. I still remember, when I was about eight, whining that I was bored. She packed me into the car and took me to the library, and I've not been bored since. She read them all: Austen, Dickens, Thackeray, Ross Macdonald, Ruth Rendell, Fielding. There was no close analysis of text, no lit crit: she loved the stories, and she read for pleasure.

I guess my brother and I get our almost total lack of ambition from her: she just wanted to have fun, to go through life seeing new things, learning about what interested her, going to new places. Because of this, I went through life never having a real job, never having a pension plan, never settling down in one place or at one job, but having an enormous amount of fun. If this lack of seriousness in her child distressed her, she certainly never gave any sign of it.

She loved a joke, loved a pun, was happiest when making other people laugh. The foibles of mankind were a source of infinite delight to her: she loved a hypocrite, could not resist a fool, treasured the pronouncements of a bore. She was a gifted mimic and spared no one: the next-door neighbour came alive in a gesture or word, and no Sunday sermon that lasted more than ten minutes would pass unglossed.

That my brother and I survived our childhood without developing rickets or beriberi and without growing to the size of baby hippopotamuses is evidence of divine intervention. Irish mother + German father = meat and potatoes. Vegetables – and here I must draw a veil of silence over my childhood memories – came from a can or a frozen rectangle. Perhaps the fruit saved us, for she loved fresh fruit and the house was always overflowing with apples, peaches, strawberries, bananas, but I never saw a zucchini until I was in my forties. Garlic? Pasta? Are you kidding?

She had the metabolism of a sixteen-year-old boy and remained thin, though she ate like a shark. Part of that had to do, I suppose, with the fact that unless she was sitting and reading, she was in motion. She played tennis well into her seventies, always walked and moved quickly, as though in a hurry to get to the next thing and do it.

It's the business of mothers to love their kids. We were lucky that she also liked us, and this was a feeling we reciprocated entirely. She was a sweet-tempered woman and never tried to threaten us into doing things or not doing things. That we both ended up pretty shiftless and utterly devoid of a life plan or Higher Purpose is her doing. Bless her.

Stubborn as a mule – well, stubborn as Grumpy – she could seldom be shifted from an opinion once she'd formed it. Her responses to people were immediate and visceral, and she seldom pulled back from initial approval or dislike. Luckily, she was seldom wrong. If asked about these opinions, she never provided an explanation: she'd shrug, and that was the way things were going to remain. She could be, and was, kidded about her obstinacy, but she could never be made to give it up.

She died of emphysema, so the cigarettes got her. But she held out until her eighties. The week before she died, we talked, as we'd been doing for ages, about this and that. At one point, she said, 'I'm tired of this,' and then she smiled. A week later, when the phone rang at three in the morning – it always rings at three in the morning, doesn't it? – I knew it would be my brother, and I was right.

Well, she had a good run, and she had a lot of fun, and she left behind a lot of people who love her still and remember her, always, with endless affection and amusement. Not bad, was it?

Part Two:
On the Road

11. Drugs, Sex, and Rock 'n' Roll

During one of the protracted periods of disoccupation with which my life has been filled, I read an ad in the *New York Times* offering jobs in Iran for teachers of English. It was, if memory serves, 1976, which puts me in my early thirties, and I knew about Iran only that it had formerly been called Persia – which certainly has a magical sound – and that it was the site of Persepolis and the Meidan-e Shah mosque in Isfahan. Beyond that, I knew it was near Afghanistan, not that I had a clear idea of the whereabouts of that country.

I sent off a letter and filled out an application that was returned by post, and a month later I landed in Isfahan, an employee of a company called Telemedia, which I learned in my first week was called Tell 'em Anything by its employees.

I had read a bit about the country and its customs, but little had prepared me for my first sight of downtown Isfahan: a parade of men in bloody white shirts walking closely together through the city, flailing at their backs with nail-studded chains, hence the blood. I'd been to Spain and seen the Good Friday flagellations, so I recognized this instantly as a religious manifestation.

Two days later, I started teaching – get ready – basic English to members of the Iranian Air Force who were training to be helicopter pilots. They studied in the language programme for thirty-six weeks, if I recall correctly, and then progressed to flight school, where a ragtag group of former US Army and Air Force pilots taught them the rudiments and finer points of helicopter flight. The foreign pilots and mechanics spoke only English, so our cadets had to master English before entering flight school.

It took me just a month to realize that I did not want to spend the next year or years teaching young men to say, 'The book is red.' Nor was I much attracted to the idea that, with my help, they would progress to, 'I am getting ready for lift-off, sir.'

A friend with whom I had started to play tennis after work asked if I'd like to transfer to his department, 'Testing', about which I knew little. 'It would give us more time for tennis,' he said in encouragement, and I suddenly knew as much about 'Testing' as I needed to know. The decision made itself: Testing it was.

This meant that instead of teaching six forty-minute classes a day, and giving and correcting homework, I would instead work on the third floor (view of the airfield) and have the key to a locker into which I could put my tennis whites and racquet.

The tests had to be written to suit each week's instructional programme, corrected, and then evaluated to see what the students were and were not learning. I was assigned to writing tests, so it became my task to ask the students which was correct: 'I am wanting to become a pilot' or 'I want to become a pilot.' Gentle reader, please do not suspect that the creation of such sentences did not require a great deal of thought: I'm sure Proust began with equally simple decisions.

Another two weeks passed before my friend suggested that we play a little tennis after our work shift. So we began, and because it was such a pleasant way to spend our free hours, each day we shaved a few more minutes from work time and added them to our time on the courts.

By the end of my first year, my schedule had intensified, so I arrived at work at eight and left to play tennis at nine, returning at one, but only to change from my whites, hide my racquet, and return to the office with a sheaf of papers under my arm, announcing that 'Headquarters was satisfied with the new tests.'

By then, it was evident that I could not be trusted with the invention of questions; indeed, it was evident that I did not grasp the seriousness of our teaching mission. The proof? 'Which is more important to transportation, the helicopter or the camel?' 'Where is the toilet located in the 201 helicopter?' 'Why are there no parachutes in helicopters?' My absence from the office was more applauded than criticized.

I also learned, observing and talking to my colleagues, that in this expatriate world there were few rules about social behaviour. So long as one paid one's share of the bill after having a drink or a meal, society was there to be enjoyed. It was not done to criticize or condemn the teaching methods of a colleague, nor was criticism of someone's personal choices accepted. In short, so long as a person was discreet and polite, not much else mattered.

During the next few years, my tennis game improved, until I won – and I say this with pride – the Pahlavi Cup for women's singles for the entire city of Isfahan. There were, to the best of my understanding, six other Western women in Isfahan who played tennis, perhaps two hours a week, on Sundays: I wiped the courts with them.

New teachers continued to arrive from the States, but as time passed the supply diminished, and the company began to hire people who had stumbled off the Drug Bus that ran between Munich and Kabul or who had run out of money in Tehran. Young Americans or Brits invented university degrees, got a job teaching English, and stayed until they hit the road again.

My favorite of them was a woman who earned the name 'Broken Nancy', Nancy because it was her first name and 'Broken' because, during her first week at work, she jumped into an empty swimming pool and broke her leg. She was also spectacularly incompetent as a teacher: she once dropped a photo and replaced it in the wrong sequence, then went for eight weeks without realizing that when she projected a photo of an altimeter on the screen, she told the students that it was the main rotor, and when she showed them the right pedal, she told them it was the cockpit. American hubris can perhaps be blamed for the military debacle of Iran. Bear in mind, however, that my colleagues and

I in no way contributed to the war effort on the part of the Shah's army.

The view from our office showed us the far-off hills but also the landing field where our cadets took their practical exams, often a year after leaving our skilled tutelage. We sometimes watched the flight exams of our former students: a helicopter rose from the ground, nose down, tail waving back and forth in the manner of a happy puppy. It turned brusquely to the right and continued in a full circle. The turning stopped, and it nodded a few times, as if to confirm that it had indeed intended to spin around in a cheerful circle. Then, raising its proud head, it raced towards the finish line in the manner of a rocking horse, the rear rotor a ter-rifying hair's breadth from the ground. Wobbling a bit, as if in the grip of some sort of mechanical palsy, it landed at the finish line and shuddered to a halt.

Perhaps thirty seconds passed, whereupon the heli-copter, now answering the commands of the American pilot, rose in a stiff horizontal position and flew back in a straight line before landing softly in the same place from which the student had removed it.

The students were respectful and pleasant, eager to learn and to succeed. Many came to us illiterate in Farsi: English was the first language they learned to read. Many of them had never driven a car when they began their classes. They were sweet boys, soon to be swept up and away by events over which they had no control.

The serpent always lurks outside the garden, does it not? Find a peaceful life, and soon Destiny will inter-fere. So it proved for Persia, and, by extension, all of us in the employ of Telemedia.

Many people have written about the Islamic Revolution, I know, and I'd like to add my bit. To the best of my knowledge, there was no anti-American feeling manifest at the beginning. Our Persian neighbours came to our door during the period of martial law and told us that the rumours were saying the water in the city had been poisoned, and if we wanted any, we should come and get it from them. Our colleagues often spoke of the concern their Persian neighbours showed for them, of their offers of food or shelter.

Strangely enough, although we lived under martial law during the final months of 1978 and the first few months of 1979, I never felt a sense of menace. Our neighbours were polite and friendly. The people from whom we bought yogurt, bread, eggs, vegetables, and fruit still smiled and nodded when we visited their shops; taxi drivers still took us where we needed to go; the bank was open and willing to give us cash. Our landlord made it clear that he wanted us to stay on as his tenants; he even planted more geraniums – horrible flowers – in the garden, and we thanked him effusively and offered him tea.

Thus a new social event was born: the curfew pyjama party. The curfew was imposed by whatever authority remained in the city: everyone was to be off the streets at dark. It was winter, so 'dark' was a vague phenomenon that occurred sometime between five and, if you pushed at your imagination, six-thirty. We were meant to leave work at four, so this left us little time to get back to the city, buy food or run errands, or visit friends. And we simply forgot, so we'd stop for a drink or a coffee or tea at a friend's house, and only

when we heard a burst of gunfire would we look outside and see that it was already dark.

A few people did get stopped by men in uniform,
although it was never entirely clear what they were or
where on the Shah–Ayatollah spectrum they stood.
One friend was taken to a police station, given some
supper, and put alone in a cell – with clean bedding –
for the night, then taken to a cab at dawn.

After a time, people offered to be hosts for the curfew pyjama parties, usually people who lived in
enormous old Qajar houses with eight or ten rooms.
Persians have an innate delicacy of behaviour, and so
women were never searched. This made it easy to
carry a change of underwear and perhaps pyjamas
when leaving for work.

I believe that, during the period when more than
fifty thousand Americans left the country, only two
were killed, but that was information passed on by
rumour: I do not know if any Americans died.

In the early months of 1979, we were still there, still
employed, still being paid, although the students had
evaporated, and it was evident the game would soon
be over. Telemedia (the US government having
washed its hands of us) tried to find planes that
would take us from Iran. Until that time, we were all
moved to a housing development being built outside
the city and meant to be inhabited by the foreign
community as part of the American government's
long-term plans for continued activity in Iran. One-
storey houses with sloped roofs, lots of space, and
green lawns with grass that was likely to be sun-
burned into straw within a week: all this was ours.
Tennis courts, community centre, swimming pool,

sports fields, gymnasium, garages. Close your eyes and you were in Southern California.

Once the idea sank in that the gig was up, those people who used drugs began in earnest to use whatever they had in store while they still could, no one being brave enough to think of sending it back home. The Class Six liquor store on the US military base had a going-out-of-business sale and slashed the prices on beer, wine, and alcohol, so the drinkers hit lucky too, and began to try to drink the place dry.

Because I'd never cultivated a taste for drugs, I was left playing endless sets of tennis and perhaps having a beer after we finished. The reckless abandon of the druggies and the drinkers was matched only by our profligacy in the use of tennis balls. There must have been hundreds of boxes containing cans of tennis balls in the military sports shop: thousands of balls, and the guys from the shop left them all beside the courts for us. The builders had not managed to get the fences put up around the tennis courts before the tanks moved into the city, so we simply let the missed balls run off into the dying grass beyond the courts. This meant that twelve, fifteen cans could be used to play a few sets of singles. Seen from high enough above, it might have looked like an early videogame, with hundreds of white dots spread around a clay-colored rectangle.

Two hallucinogenic events stand at different points in my memories: the comic and the frightening.

My immediate boss took seriously the imperative to consume all available drugs before leaving the country. To do this, he remained drugged, on opium, most of his waking hours. Thus it was that I sat across from him (substituting for my tennis pal that day, who was busy with a tournament) as he explained to the Boss of Bosses, a former colonel in the US Army who insisted on being addressed by his rank and not his name, the Testing Department's plans for the future. This meeting took place in a large room on the Persian airbase where we worked and where we had arrived that day on the bright yellow Blue Bird school bus that took us back and forth between the city and the base. The streets we passed on the way were littered with machine-gun shell casings, burned-out cars, tanks, and burning tyres. It was evident that the Americans were on the losing side, and we'd begun to worry about when, and how, we'd get out of there.

The colonel, however, seemed not to have considered this possibility and was thus busy enquiring about next year's educational programme. My boss had arrived at the meeting to explain just that and carried a thick folder filled with documents and a small silver pillbox. He set the papers in front of him, the pillbox to the right. Before he spoke, he opened the folder and pulled out copies of next year's plan. He opened the pillbox and pushed the contents around with his finger, as though searching for an aspirin among the sleeping pills.

I took a closer look and saw that he was, instead, poking about in the box in search of a piece of opium just the right size to get him through the meeting: not too big and not too small, but just right. When he found it, he put it in his mouth and began to suck on it as though it were a piece of candy, then he picked up the copies and passed them to the people around the table.

As the room grew quiet, we could better hear the sound of gunshots, interspersed with the occasional explosion, from the city, about three kilometres away. There was also the frequent sound of planes taking off. No landings.

Once everyone had a copy of the plan, the director of Testing began to explain it: in March, the vocabulary list would expand to include newer types of aircraft. In April, there would be a graduation ceremony for one entire class. And in July, we would have a visit from the Minister of Defence, plans for which were already being made.

Poke, poke, prod, and he slipped another small piece of opium into his mouth, swallowed it, and said, 'And then in November, we'd like a day off so that we could celebrate Thanksgiving at home.'

No one laughed. No one whispered. No one jumped to his feet, screaming, 'You're crazy. We're all crazy.' We all sat quietly, and my suspicion was enforced that we had best not anticipate that free turkey.

A few weeks later, we were informed to prepare for 'departure'. The word 'evacuation' was not used. Undescribed, unnamed vehicles would pick up the teaching and administrative staff that remained, at midnight, and we would drive through the night to Tehran, there to be flown from the country.

Leaving my racquet behind, I packed everything I owned into three large suitcases and abandoned them there, 'to be shipped at a later date'. I included the final draft of my doctoral dissertation, 'The Changing Moral Order in the World of Jane Austen's Novels', which I'd been working on while in Iran, and went to the meeting point a quarter of an hour early. I remember that it was cold, and few people spoke.

Precisely at midnight, a number of yellow Blue Bird school buses pulled into the parking lot of the housing development, and we filed on silently, stuffing our carry-on bags in the racks above us.

Few jokes, little conversation, and that in soft voices. The yellow caravan left quietly. Sometime in the night, I came awake when the motor of the bus slowed, then stopped. In front of us, illuminated by our headlights, a truck was parked perpendicular to the road, blocking traffic. The Blue Bird opened its wing and three young men climbed on board. The first held a flashlight. He came down the aisle of the bus, stopping at each row and, one by one, shining the light into the startled faces that slowly turned towards him.

It was not until he arrived at the row where I was sitting by the window that I could see that the other two men were close behind him, each carefully pointing his machine gun into each newly revealed face.

In normal circumstances – which no longer existed – this would have been terrifying. These boys – and they were boys, could easily have been our students – had been given a job to do, and they were doing it. It did not occur to us that the guns were meant as anything but stage props; the search of the bus was something they'd seen in movies and so thought they had to do. No one gasped, no one panicked, and no one spoke.

When they reached the back of the bus, they turned round and walked to the front. Before they got off, the one with the flashlight turned back and said, *'Khoda hafez,'* the polite way to say 'goodbye'.

We reached Tehran and were flown out the next day. Five months later, the three suitcases showed up. The Iranians had stolen nothing, but they had confiscated all documents: tax records, letters, books, even doctoral dissertations. For some time, I fantasized about an Iranian customs inspector pulling out what was certain to be a handbook on spy techniques and asking a colleague, 'Akbar, what is *Mansfield Park*?'

But I'd decided not to continue my studies. Besides, I had started to think about looking for a new job.

12. Odd Job

With the disappearance of my job in Iran, I was unemployed, and so I thought it might be interesting to have a bit of a vacation. Thus, I spent three months using a round-the-world ticket on Pan Am to do just that, going east from New York and stopping when and where I liked, so long as I stayed on Pan Am and kept going east.

Returning from the trip, I began trying to find a teaching job somewhere. *Mirabile dictu*, China answered, offering me a year's contract as a professor of English literature at the University of Suzhou, a hundred miles west of Shanghai, which I accepted. In 1979, Suzhou was a small city with a population of about half a million (today it is around 10 million), known as 'the Venice of the Orient'. (There was a canal.)

At some time in its past, the university had been a mission school run by a Christian church; now it was a training ground for future teachers of English. Also teaching there was another American woman who had a master's degree in English and was appointed half the teaching. I had told 'the leaders', as they were ever called, that I'd not finished my dissertation, but they had chosen to ignore this. I was thus both a PhD and a 'foreign expert' and so was assigned to teach English literature to the Chinese professors who were finishing their master's degrees and to have a more limited contact with the university students working towards their first degree.

Almost four years living and teaching in Iran had taught me the wisdom of showing appreciation of and respect for local customs. I'd also learned to keep my mouth shut, to nod and smile at what was said or explained to me, and, at all costs, to avoid any reference to religion or politics.

Because we were 'foreign experts', we were treated with respect and given a house to live in, along with a maid, a cook, a man of all work, and our two translators, young women students who spoke good English. One of them mentioned that her parents were members of the Party, and the other added, finding it difficult to disguise her pride, that her parents were as well.

We arrived in late September, just in time for the first term. I had a light teaching schedule, two classes a day, one for the senior-year students and one for my colleagues, the Chinese teachers working towards their advanced degrees. Once a month, as well, each of us was asked to give a talk about life in the United States.

The students were attentive and respectful and knew that their future was in our hands: the better their grade in our classes, the more likely would be their chance at a job in a city and not in 'the country-side', which they made sound like a suburb of hell. The same was probably true for our Chinese colleagues.

It always takes time to adjust to new surroundings, but China proved more difficult than any of the other places I'd lived. We were perpetually gawked at, for the people of Suzhou had not seen foreigners for decades, many of them never in their lives. Their astonishment was never troublesome in any way; whenever we got lost while riding around on our faithful Flying Pigeon bicycles, hand signals, even shepherding, were gladly provided to get us on the way back to the campus. But this did not stop the people we encountered from crowding around us and sometimes pointing to our enormous noses and odd-colored hair.

We asked our translators to teach us some basic Chinese, but our difficulty in distinguishing the difference between the tones tossed us back to asking to be taught a few sentences and key words. I soon realized that we were thus dependent upon the two daughters of Communist Party members for the translation of all we said to or heard from students or people on the street. I also noticed the coolness that existed between our two translators and the other students. The third penny to drop was the repeated appearance of one or both of the translators any time we could be heard going down the steps of the house in which we all lived, hoping to pass out of the door and then off-campus on our own. They wanted, of course, to help us. I can still walk down a wooden staircase making less noise than a mouse, and there does not exist a door that I cannot open silently.

Contacts with the students sometimes revealed interesting prejudices: Black authors were confusing because of my students' certainty that Black people were inferior. How, then, could what they wrote be worth reading? Hotel rooms, I learned, were cleaned with great severity after a Black tourist had stayed there, and once a Chinese woman had had sex with a Black man, she ran the risk of giving birth to a half-Black child at any time in her life. And Jews, they were quick to inform me, were greedy and dishonest, something I'd never known before.

Since I didn't know any of this, I asked the students how it was that they – who had never been beyond the borders of their province and had never seen a Black person even from a distance, nor a Jew – did. Much to our surprise, and my embarrassment, I discovered that it was most likely the result of what they'd read from anglophone writers.

That settled, they illuminated me with the information that Tibetans, some of whom one or two of the students had actually seen, were not really human, but only one step ahead of animals, and some of them doubted even that.

I was not prepared for their nervous response to some of the love sonnets of Shakespeare and Donne, but it was not until one of them suggested, 'Perhaps there is too much mention of sex in these poems,' that I realized the folly of my reading choices. We switched immediately to the nature poetry of the Romantics and all went well.

After some time, my teaching and my conversation became as bland as vanilla pudding: there was some substance, but no spice, nothing new, nothing nourishing. Read the poem and give a literal, word-by-word translation; don't bother with a second meaning or an ambiguous word. Passion? Beauty? Danger? In poetry? Are you mad? Occasionally, I'd ask them to read one of Shakespeare's easier sonnets, 'My mistress' eyes', for example, and delight in those who understood the poet's joke, leaving those who did not to utter confusion.

The students, I soon realized, had little interest in the larger world. They displayed no curiosity about the United States, save for once, when I was asked to explain this famous thing, 'the Stock Market', in one of my monthly lectures. And did. Silence fell upon the room as I tried to explain the idea of private property and a private company and the possibility of buying a part of it in the form of stock in the company. And thus profit without working for it. I once attended the feast of the Liquefaction of the Blood of San Gennaro in the cathedral of Naples and was awestruck at the radiant faith and mystical silence of the people assembled to observe the miracle. Only in that classroom in China have I sensed a similar manifestation of Faith in the Divine.

There were moments of delight: weekends in Shanghai, staying in a hotel; seeing the rather boring statues in Xi'an, the caves of Dunhuang; the Forbidden City. But I'm a bad tourist, and it was always the tiny, all but invisible things that snapped me to attention. After we'd been there six months or so, the English-language

newspaper carried articles about a breakout of encephalitis in Shanghai and recommended that foreigners get
the vaccine, available in that city. We, of course, had to
request permission for this from 'the leaders', those
omnipotent deciders of where we could and could not
go. With one of our translators, we went to the large
office of the 'leader' and made our request, explaining
the seriousness of both the news articles and the
disease.

The 'leader', who was shocked both by the name of
the disease and by our request, rose in his chair, scandalized by such a proposal, and hotly denied that
encephalitis existed in China. We left, a bit confused,
not so much by the decision as by his horror, one might
say disgust, at our request. As we walked across the
campus, the heavens opened and an angelic voice
whispered the word 'syphilis' in my ear, just as some
Confucian version of that angel had whispered 'syphilis' in the 'leader's' ear.

So I played the scene again: two unaccompanied
Western women, worried about the possibility that
they were going to contract syphilis, asking permission to go to Shanghai for a weekend.

Before the winter holiday, I requested permission to
go to Lhasa, since there was already a flight from
Shanghai to the Tibetan capital. When, as I knew
would happen, my request was refused, I asked for an
explanation. Concern for my safety sounded in the
voice of the 'leader', who told me that there had been
heavy rains in the north-west, and the roads were
blocked. I had no choice but to smile warmly and
thank him for his concern for my safety on the road.

The last little thing that I stored in my memory, well, stored it twice, for it was told to me two times, was a remark made by two of the people I met there. Both told me that they had never, in all their lives, spoken to anyone as openly as they had to me about China and what it was like to live there.

And even now, forty years later, I still feel a faint nervousness that the 'leaders' will find out what they said to me and who they are.

13. $audiopoly

It's said that prisoners must keep busy in order to avoid going mad. Using crumbs and shreds of apple peel, soft voices and never a sudden move, they spend months luring mice into friendship. The Birdman of Alcatraz devoted his solitude to the study of birds and became famous in the process. I've no idea what the Man in the Iron Mask did to keep himself from running mad – oil his jaw, perhaps. In the early 1980s, imprisoned in the Kingdom of Saudi Arabia, sentenced to an academic year by having signed a one-year contract to teach women students at King Saud University in Riyadh, I found myself in a similar situation, though my prison was a four-room apartment in a modern complex, and thus no mice, and no birds.

In the absence of these transient friends and with no need to oil my jaw, time weighed heavily upon me, as it did upon friends who lived in the same fenced compound. There was no alcohol (that existed only in the homes of Saudis or in the distilleries run in the compounds of foreign companies) and the use of drugs (in which I've never taken any interest, anyway) was punishable by death. There was squash, there was swimming, there was the gold bazaar: befriending a mouse seemed a more interesting option.

I no longer remember where the idea originated, nor whose it was, but one day three of us teachers decided that it might be amusing, and diverting, to create a board game with which to while away our long hours of non-working time. I know I was responsible for the invention of the name, $audiopoly, and I remain, decades later, wildly proud of that moment of inspiration, as I am of the subtitle I added to the outside of the playing board: 'A Bored Game'.

As the title shows, we were inspired – though Colin was English and Karen from New Zealand – by that monument to American capitalism, that four-cornered hymn to buying and selling and owning and amassing: Monopoly. In our separate countries, using games where the prime pieces of property bore different names, we had nonetheless learned that the blue places were best, and all of us knew in our bones that the best protection life would ever offer us was a Get Out of Jail Free card.

The entire project, if memory serves, took us about three months: we were university professors, after all, and had our professional duties to attend to. As time passed and the creation of the game became our compelling obsession, teaching became an ever more irritating obstacle, at least until we discovered various ways of disguising work on $audiopoly as the teaching of English literature or medicine. Working at the photocopier, sitting for long periods of time gazing off into space, suddenly exclaiming at the discovery of the absolutely correct phrase: surely, all of these were necessary parts of the teaching process, were they not?

But before all of that, we needed an overall goal for the game; one might even call it a philosophy. What desire could possibly be so strong as to compel adults to spend hours pushing little figures back and forth along the four sides of a board? What holy grail would unite these three crusaders, what common goal would inspire anyone and everyone who played $audiopoly? What is it that any foreigner who spends time in Saudi Arabia most wants, desires, lusts after? The answer to that was revealed on Square 40, the space upon which one had to land in order to win the game, assuming, that is, that the person had accumulated sufficient wealth and had eluded the snares and dangers built into the game. To land on Square 40 was to attain that ultimate of desires, for to land on Square 40 was to 'Clear Saudi Airspace'.

Now let me tell you how we got there. The board was easy: one needed only to transpose Boardwalk and Park Place to corresponding places in Riyadh. The utilities quickly became Al Rajhi, the money-changing office, and Euromarché and Panda, the two main supermarkets.

Jail? What could be the equivalent of Jail? By then, we had been sufficiently mauled by the cogs and wheels of the university administration to have developed a healthy contempt for it, and for them. Thus Jail

had to be 'Administration', the office that had confiscated our passports upon our arrival and proved
resistant to all our efforts to have them back; the office
that routinely made errors in our pay cheques; the
office that continually changed the rules governing
our employment. Thus to go to Administration was to
languish unseen, unaided, and unheard.

None of us, alas, had thought to bring a game of
Monopoly with us to the Kingdom, nor were we able
to find a copy of the game, neither among friends nor
in any of the stores in Riyadh. Thus we were forced to
construct ours from memory. Wasn't there something
about Good Luck cards? And Chance cards? A friend
of ours who spoke Arabic told us that there were at
least two forms of luck in Arab culture, *haz* and *karam*,
one of them good luck and one of them blind luck, but
I now forget which is which. The *Karam* and *Haz* cards
I still have suggest that it's *haz* that will always bless
you, while *karam* tosses you up in the air, a victim of
the winds of chance.

The absence of a Monopoly board to copy was but
the first obstacle to our desire to use more actual place
names on the board; the other, and more compelling,
was the realization that, were we to own property in
Riyadh – however imaginary that ownership or that
property might be – we might slip into the delusion
that we had some stake in the place, might grow
attached to it. Further, since the purpose of the game
was to 'Clear Saudi Airspace', the last thing the game
should provide was the ownership of property.

The overriding purpose of the game, anyway, was
motion, not stability. One had to keep moving around

the board, going forward and back, according to what Chance decreed, always in hopes of landing on that elusive, that lucky, that heavenly Square 40.

The way to Square 40 was as fraught with difficulty and impediments as the soul's path to Paradise. As all of us were in the Kingdom for that most base of motives, greed – there is no other reason to go – it was imperative that the person passing through Square 40 and off to freedom take with them an adequate supply of money. Since we had been in the Kingdom for at least four months by the time we began working on the game, we all knew there was no 'adequate' compensation for our time spent there, so at the very least the sum had to be enormous. Wealth was available to players in the form of Saudi riyals or gold, the price of which fluctuated wildly during the length of the game.

Play began for all players at the Riyadh Airport, and each player was given 4,000 riyals at the beginning of the game. Every time a player passed through the airport, they received another 4,000 riyals, equal to a month's salary. Regardless of how much money or gold a player had accumulated during play, he or she was obliged to pay a bribe of 10,000 riyals to the customs authorities in order to leave the country. Well worth it.

Gold, that shining symbol of avarice, played an important function in the game, for as well as the 10,000 riyals that had to be paid to get out of the place, it was also necessary to pay five ounces of gold (equally well spent). To mirror the precarious nature of fortune, the price of gold, which began the game at 2,400 riyals an ounce, rose and fell 400 riyals an ounce, depending upon which squares players landed on. Thus a person who spent much of the game amassing a fortune in gold could be beggared in the twinkling of an eye, just as easily as he or she could be catapulted to sudden wealth by a more favorable roll of the dice. Round and round the board the players were propelled by the dice.

Perhaps it is time to talk of the tiny pieces available to the players. There was the whisky truck, the hazardous-waste truck, the earth-moving machine, the racing car, and the gold transportation truck used to bring the bars to and from the bank. All of these tiny pieces, I boast proudly, were the result of my genius; I spent hours at my desk at the university, transforming erasers, matchboxes, and bottles of Wite-Out into vehicles, their wheels made of buttons and garment snaps.

In order to test their board worthiness, I spent hours running them back and forth on the top of my desk, much to the consternation of my colleagues and students. Since women were then not allowed to drive in Saudi Arabia, this was as close as I came to exercising control over a vehicle for nine months.

When questioned about the cars and trucks, I smilingly explained that it was a form of therapy to keep me from becoming violent and killing someone. It had early become law to us that no one – and that meant *no one* – was to learn about $audiopoly, for to have been discovered at it would probably have led to our arrest, certainly to our deportation.

The reason for that lies in the content. So far, I have not mentioned the texts of the squares other than

Blessed 40, nor have I quoted the texts of the *Haz* and *Karam* cards. Perhaps it is best to do so, if only for a few, so as to make it clear why we worked only at home and only behind locked doors.

Chosen at random, some of the *Haz* cards read: 'Inadvertently give failing grade to member of Royal Family. Lose one week's salary.' It was not done to give failing grades to students. They might be lazy, they might be stupid, they might be both, but it was made sufficiently clear that no one was to fail. Even less possible was the idea that a member of any one of a number of wealthy or well-connected families might be shown to be the idiot he or she was.

While I was there, the story circulated of the British professor of surgery at the medical school of Abdulaziz Hospital who, finding himself teaching students with less skill than a butcher, failed all of them save two Palestinians, who he said 'probably wouldn't kill anyone'. He was called, we were told, into the office of the dean of the medical school and told to change the grades because Saudi students, all of whom the failed students were, could not fail a class.

One thinks here of the triumphant final chorus of Thomas Arne's opera *Alfred*: 'Rule Britannia, Britannia, rule the waves, Britons never, never, shall be slaves.'

Citing the Hippocratic oath he had taken upon becoming a doctor, the professor refused. He left the country that evening. The Saudi students all received passing grades in their surgery class.

Or this card: 'Caught asking for ham and cheese sandwich at Mövenpick. Fined 600 riyals.' Some of the larger companies, all of which had stills and breweries within their compounds, were also rumoured to fly in pork and bacon for their personnel. As a vegetarian, I was not privy to further details.

Or this: 'Stage *Israel in Egypt* and *Moses and Aaron* for the Riyadh Opera Company. Fined 1,000 riyals.' I suspect the inspiration for this one came from the firing and next-day deportation of a colleague who had, with a significant lack of forethought, asked the students in her English literature class to read parts of *Paradise Lost*.

There were more: 'Day off to pray for rain. Collect one day's salary.' Yes, this happened. Or this: 'Win a year's supply of camel meat.'

'Obtain patent for battery-powered Mecca finder. Earn 1,000 riyals.' Some of the students had wristwatches that, even then, had a prototype GPS and would point to Mecca no matter where the owner happened to be.

I still remember the hoots of delight with which we greeted the arrival of these ideas, and I remember how, keeping pace with our daily encounters with abuse, dishonesty, and primitive incivility, the ideas expressed on the cards escalated ever closer to open attacks on our host nation. Our only form of defence was this covert, entirely passive offence.

The game was philosophically about the acquisition of wealth, but there came a time when theory had to give way to practice, and the actual playing board, money, and pieces had to be manufactured. Our colleagues saw the photocopying machine as a means to reproduce their non-demanding homework exercises and the exams everyone was guaranteed to pass. For us, however, the photocopying machine was a mint.

All we had to do was excise the label 'Saudi Arabian Monetary Agency' from a hundred-riyal bill and replace it with '$audiopoly' and we were in business. There were a few times when hundred-riyal notes were left forgotten on the photocopying machine, but we were by then practised liars (how quickly one adopts local customs) and easily invented our way out of potentially dangerous situations.

For the rolling of the dice, we needed cups, and what better than the dear little ceramic cups, made in Japan, used for Arabic coffee and all bearing the crossed scimitars and stylized palm tree of the dear little Saud family?

We spent weeks designing prototype boards, alternating squares that allowed progress with those that condemned players to retreat. Inshallah, baby. Thus a person who landed on Square 12 – 'Admiring prince drops 3,000 riyals into your pêche Melba at Mövenpick. Upon return from weekend in Bahrain, advance three spaces' – would, upon moving ahead three spaces to Square 15, be greeted with, 'Caught not paying for public bus. Fined 500 riyals. Go to Administration.' Yes, there was a Get Out of Administration Free card, but there was only one; otherwise, the process of liberation was purest Kafka.

The player unfortunate enough to land on Square 21 was 'Caught distributing Bibles on number 7 bus. Fined 700 riyals. Lose one turn.' We had decided not to discuss flogging in the game. Square 30? 'Attempted rape by yellow cab driver. You are fined 1,000 riyals.' So much for the position of women in the Kingdom.

Did I hear you ask about the general level of medical treatment in the Kingdom? How about Square 34? 'Bus to souk involved in accident in Panda parking lot. Lose one turn or the extremity of your choice.' Or perhaps 23: 'Strange virus. Doctors dumbfounded. Go to Abdulaziz.' Let me quell your fears and assure you that, yes, there was a Get Out of Abdulaziz Alive card, the most valuable in the game.

But it was not all bad luck: who knows, sometimes good things can happen, even in the Kingdom. Just have a look at Square 9: 'Sell copy of final exam. Earn 2,000 riyals.' This square was created in homage to a colleague of ours who had set up a cottage industry writing theses for students in the Department of English Literature in the men's college: I have a clear memory of helping with one about *The Great Gatsby*, though I refused payment. More good luck awaited on Square 13: 'Find two cases of '64 Bordeaux mislabelled "Finest Non-Alcoholic Grape Juice". Win six new friends. Take *Karam* card.' The most enterprising players always longed to land on Square 36: 'Establish Riyadh Escort Service – "No Taste is too Debased".'

And so it went, for months. The unhealthy heat of winter turned into the unbearable heat of spring, and soon it was time for graduation. Just think, everyone passed their classes and everyone was promoted or graduated. Just like in America, 'No student left behind.' And then it was May and our contracts finished, and those who had not been in trouble with the morals police were invited to return to teach yet another year at King Saud University. Most of us fled. We three took with us our $audiopoly boards. I've

always wondered if our choice to fly on three succes-
sive days, and all to different continents, was in any
way related to the desire to be sure that at least one,
even if only one, $audiopoly game made it out of the
dear little Kingdom.

14. Made in the USA

After nine months in Saudi Arabia, my spirit sought peace and beauty, and so I moved to the city where those things were most abundantly to be found: Venice. I arrived without a job or the possibility of finding one legally, and thus without a future.

But then the whispering angel who has been of such help to me all through my life pronounced the words 'Caserma Ederle' in my ear. And sure enough, there it was, a United States Army base, not only an hour from Venice, but in the phone book (this was 1981) as well. The switchboard operator transferred my call to the office of the University of Maryland. Yes, indeed, a real live American university – and quite a respectable one – had the contract with the entire US military to provide university instruction and the chance of a degree to members of the US military, their family, or any civilian employee who wanted to attend classes.

And, as chance would have it, they were searching for a professor of English literature for a class that was to begin in a week, and would I like to come out and be interviewed?

A week later, our heroine began teaching that class to a group of about thirty soldiers, most of them in their twenties and a few of them actually interested in English literature; the others were there because they were required to take at least one class in 'the Humanities' before graduation. This was at a time when many young Americans, faced with the staggering cost of private education – which meant most colleges and universities – joined the military in order to defray tuition costs while also serving as a soldier. In many cases, the decision to join the military was made in the hope of earning a university degree, not from the desire to be a soldier.

I forget the exact make-up of that class: most were male and most were white, and a number of them were interested in reading something other than sports or motorcycle magazines. During the first class, I asked them what they most liked to read; after they told me, I made a quick change in the syllabus, and we began reading short stories, leaving poetry for last.

One thing that struck me early on was how extraordinarily polite they were. Most of the enlisted people seemed to come from the South and thus were raised in a culture that believed that older people and people with an education were to be treated with respect. I was also struck by how intelligent many of them were, grasping concepts and possibilities as quickly as frogs snatch up flies. They lacked only the ability to express themselves clearly.

They did not swear in class, and if the occasional profane word slipped out in the heat of discussion, their classmates instantly told them not to use it, and it was eliminated from their in-class vocabulary. But during the breaks, when they passed into the hallway to smoke and to talk among themselves, the banished words returned. They never appeared on the page of anything they wrote.

Listening to their comments and questions, I began to realize just how clever some of them were and to see clearly the difference between ignorance and stupidity. They were ignorant of many things: science, medicine, world history, geography, Italy, grammar, American history. I once had to give a short class in logic, and the classes we spent looking at logic and logical argument showed how very quickly they could find a false syllogism or spot the *post hoc ergo propter hoc* fallacy. They immediately recognized the false dilemma and pounced on the slippery slope.

Once I'd shown them how common illogical thinking was and how to detect it, they turned into hunters and started to bring their dead prey to class with them. False claims in advertising, ad hominem attacks, even remarks made by their superior officers: once they'd been taught to recognize the plumage of error, they delighted in bringing it to the ground with one shot.

One of the joys of teaching literature is the freedom it allows to talk about any subject, so long as there is a short story, novel, play, or poem that mentions it. So a class on the European novel can turn into just about anything: the professor has simply to construct the correct syllabus and ask the right questions. I'm not sure, however, if there is an appropriate answer to the question 'Why didn't Emma Bovary just go out and get a job?' And those English poets, you'd be shocked by the things *they* talked about.

As always happened, over the years they metamorphosed from students into people. There was a Black sergeant who had converted to Islam, a choice, he said, that had saved both his marriage and his life. He had a safe-deposit box in a bank 'back home' that contained a first-edition *Batman* comic book, the first *Wonder Woman*, and a 1939 *Superman*. In order to save you the time you'd spend looking for the current value of just one of them, let me reveal that the *Art Newspaper* reported that a 'near-mint' copy of the first issue of *Batman* sold at auction in 2021 for 2.2 million bucks. I repeat: perhaps ignorant, but certainly not stupid.

Though I've forgotten many of the classes I taught, I still remember other students. The brightest was a woman sergeant from some state in the American Southwest who spoke with an accent so thick it occasionally made her incomprehensible – I'm a native speaker of English and at times had difficulty understanding her – whose language blossomed and soared aloft when she wrote. She once submitted a short story as good as anything in our textbook, better than most. She presented a scene of a young woman sitting in a diner, having a cup of coffee, that brooded with a menace and human evil that chills my soul, even after more than thirty years. I've longed ever since to steal her idea, but I lack the talent to match hers and so have resisted the temptation.

Another woman student, a hard-working, heavyset Black sergeant, took a few classes with me and then disappeared into the jaws of the war in Iraq. Three years later, I bumped into her in the base library and at first failed to recognize her, for she was thin to the point of emaciation and had grown almost as pale as I.

'Miz Leon, I'm sick,' I remember her telling me when I asked what was wrong. 'You know I'm just a clerk, never held a gun in my life. They still sent me out into the field in Iraq – had to do the bookkeeping, even there. Well, while we were goin' to where they set up the office, the jeep drove past an ammunition dump that had caught fire a few days before and was still burnin'. Didn't have gas masks, so we breathed in that grey smoke for about fifteen minutes. And ever since maybe two days later, I've been sick. Keep going to the doctors, but they tell me it's all in my head. But look at me: you didn't even recognize me. And they're tellin' me I'm not sick.'

We talked for a few minutes, and she told me about her husband and her two kids, that they were worried for her but could do nothing. All I could do was hold her hand and tell her how sorry I was. I never saw her again.

Some of them, however, were horrid people. The worst was a white sergeant, a born-again Christian who wouldn't allow (notice that verb, please) his wife to work as he believed it was her duty (this time, notice the noun) to stay home and take care of their two kids, who were in preschool.

Why, just last week, I heard a rumour that my son's kindergarten teacher is a fag. Er, excuse me, miz, a homosexual. And I don't want no faggot teaching my son.

And why is that, Sergeant?

'Cause I'm afraid he'll convert him, turn him into a little faggot.

I made a humming noise of concern and asked how many hours his son spent in the company of this man, and how many other kids there were in the class.

He's got 'em three hours in the morning, four days a week, and there's about twenty kids in the class.

I made another humming noise, this one of the distinctly numerical kind.

That's about twelve hours a week, isn't it?

Yes, ma'am.

I certainly see why you'd be worried.

He relaxed and his face grew softer. *I hoped you'd understand.*

Of course I do. It must be a stunning blow to you.

Well, maybe it's not that much, ma'am, but it sure does trouble me.

And rightly so, I agreed again. Then I asked how many hours a day his equally Christian wife spent with the kids and how many he did.

Well, Lisa Mae spends the rest of the day with them, soon as they get home from school. And I'm always with 'em when I'm home.

That'd be about – I paused and made a rough estimate of the hours his sons spent with the teacher and the hours he spent in the company of his two God-fearing parents. *Well, if you think it out, he spends about twelve hours a week with his teacher, and that would leave about a hundred hours a week when he's with you and your wife.* I smiled kindly, one might even say benevolently, and added: *Except when you're all asleep.*

If you say so, ma'am.

I shook my head, my sadness evident. *I'm assuming that you and your wife are heterosexual.*

He must have thought it was a joke, so he laughed and said, hotly, *Of course.*

And you're so uncertain about it that you're afraid this man will convert your sons away from your model of heterosexuality? I sense your nervousness about how weak it must be, but perhaps you could talk to your pastor and ask his help. Or perhaps ask a doctor, but I don't want to get too personal about this. As the Italians say, 'Tra moglie e marito, non mettere il ditto.'

Seeing his face move from confusion towards rage, I generously supplied the translation, *'Never put a finger between a wife and a husband,'* wished him a pleasant day and went about my business.

It was the only time in almost ten years working with these students that I allowed myself to insult one of them. I think it was his using the mask of Christian piety to disguise his prejudice that angered me so.

There was another, somewhat similar incident a few years later, this one with a large and lovely Black soldier, so vibrant was her spirit, so patent her kindness and humanity.

During the break, another student mentioned that her sister had had an abortion, and the first soldier launched into a semi-sermon against abortion. It was sinful, it was against God's will, it was this and it was that. I had remained in the classroom, so could not help hearing their conversation, but said nothing because it was none of my business.

The first student went silent for at least a minute, then asked, *Honey, you got a daughter who's about ten, don't you?*

Yes.

Well, whatcha gonna do if, about five, six years from now, she comes to you and tells you she's pregnant? Her friend paused and smiled fondly at her. *And you never stop tellin' me how she's gonna go to high school and you'll kill her if she don't go to university, too? Whatcha gonna do?*

The soldier opened her mouth to speak but nothing came out. Her silence spread out as far as her friend's had. At last, she nodded a few times and said, *I don't know.* The other students started to come back into the classroom, so I heard no more of the conversation.

Over the years, the students and I discovered that we liked one another. We also realized that a more difficult thing had taken place: we'd learned to respect one another. Most of them came from backgrounds where my political and social ideas were either unknown or mocked; many of their ideas and beliefs stunned me. But we had somehow come to the silent agreement that we would at least listen to the other person and let them finish saying what they thought. Some of us moved away from the received certainties we had of the other class – for it was all about class in the end, I fear – and saw the wit and humour, patience and decency in the other.

One difference remained, however: I came to realize that most of them probably believed it would be their duty to save my life, even at the cost of their own. I doubt that I, even with all the things I knew and all the books I'd read, would have been willing to do the same.

Part Three:
Italy

15. *Italia, Ti Amo*

It's true, but I don't want to live with you any more. We had about fifty wonderful years together, didn't we, from the first time I saw you from the deck of the *Leonardo da Vinci* in the late sixties, as we steamed into the harbour of Naples? How strange, that ships should play a part both in my falling in love and with my asking for a divorce, but I don't want to share you with cruise ships, nor with thirty million tourists a year. So, *ciao bella*, and you're still the love of my life.

My blood is half Irish, a quarter Latin American, and a quarter German. Not a trace of Italian blood, Italian anything, there. I was raised in New Jersey in an entirely conventional family. A few years after university, an Italian-American friend, a former university classmate, called me out of the blue, asking me if I would go along to Italy with her because her mother would not permit her to go alone to study painting: she had to find a sort of chaperone.

I was working in New York at a job that was boring, so I agreed, and a month later we were on the way. I'd known Anita, though not well, at university, but I certainly knew no other Italians, nor did I speak a word of the language.

We arrived in Naples, were met at the port by the son of a cousin of Anita's mother who, it turned out, had not been informed that Anita was bringing along a chaper— er, a friend. This made not a bit of difference, Salvatore explained as he piled our suitcases into his Fiat 600 to drive us back to Caposele, in the province of Avellino, from where Anita's mother had emigrated thirty or so years before.

The entire village had apparently been alerted to Anita's arrival, or else a lot of people just happened to walk out into the main piazza that afternoon at about five. 'Have a rest, have a rest.'

At eight, we were invited to dinner, and it was then that I fell in love with them, the whole lot of them: the villagers of Caposele, the population of the provincia d'Avellino, Southern Italians, all Italians. For there was a meal such as I'd not seen in my life, though since then I have seen many similar. Salami, sausage, pasta, chicken, green vegetables, tomatoes, salad, wine, bread, and then cheese on a platter the size of an inner tube.

More importantly, with each course was served warmth and open hospitality, the desire that we be made happy, and a festival of hands touching arms and faces, kissing, embracing, patting, as if the sense of touch was to get its fair share of the happiness at the table.

I started then to learn Italian, figuring out what *'Mangia, mangia'* meant, listening for words that were frequently repeated – *buono, ancora, pollo, bella, cugina, forchetta, coltello, bicchiere, piatto,* and then *stanca, lungo, viaggio, dormire.*

It was a bit like *Alice in Wonderland:* I was in a place where I did not understand much except that I knew I liked it. I had my first cappuccino, my first plate of pasta with vegetables that came from the garden, bread that had been baked that morning, wine from the grapes at the back of the house. To an American raised on white bread and peanut butter, accustomed to steak and canned green beans, this was Fairy Land, Wonder Land; this was, indeed, Paradise.

After two weeks there, we took a train to Rome and found rooms in a pensione. Anita started school, and I began to learn this soft, sweet language, spent time sitting in piazzas and talking to strangers. I had a guidebook, and every day I saw a church or a museum, but chiefly I walked through the city for hours, stunned by beauty, and then sat in different piazzas until someone asked to sit beside me and began to talk.

People were well dressed, unfailingly polite, eager to help me with vocabulary or pronunciation or to walk me to their favorite church or *palazzo* and then walk through it with me, telling me the secret things to look for, the hidden beauty to the left of the angel's wing.

It became entirely normal to spend my days with strangers, chatting idly about this or that, each week widening my vocabulary. Little old ladies invited me home for tea, other people told me where I could find a shoemaker. No one seemed in a hurry about any-thing, and everyone seemed pleased that a foreigner could be so interested in what they had to say.

After six months of this, Anita, who had already met the man she would eventually marry, suggested we go to Sicily. We hitch-hiked. Both ways. During the trip, we were taken into people's homes, in all cases introduced to the mother of the house, and often were taken out of the way by the driver, who wanted to show us a castle or a church we otherwise would not have seen.

In retrospect, I suspect that many people felt protect-ive of these two daffy girls, hitch-hiking their way down to Sicily and back. By taking us home to mamma, perhaps they wanted to keep us safe from what else might be driving north or south. They needn't have worried about that: at no time was either of us ever subjected to a suggestive word, an indelicate question. Or perhaps it was simply the luck of the ignorant, rather than of the innocent.

When I returned to the States – my money had run out – I realized how I'd been changed by a year among these generous, open, forgiving, patient people. No one had cheated me, no one had tried in any way to take advantage of me. I'd learned to speak their lan-guage and learned to respect their ways.

During the next few years, I was in and out of Italy like an otter in a pond until the early eighties, when I found a job and decided to settle in Venice, where I had acquired familial obligations and profound friend-ships. My luck had held, and I'd known only grace and charity from these people.

I've learned a bit about them and been enriched by their virtues: charity, generosity, love of beauty, *bella figura*, reluctance to make judgements about people, and their everlasting willingness to forgive.

Italia, ti amo.

16. The Perfect Cappuccino

You'd think that finding the perfect cappuccino in Venice would be an easy enough thing to do: just go into a bar or a *pasticceria* and ask for one. But no, in Venice nothing is easy, not bringing home six bottles of mineral water, nor finding a plumber, nor finding the perfect cappuccino.

At the end of the nineties, when I moved to a new apartment, I started to go to Didovich in Campo Santa Marina: the brioche were glorious and the cappuccino acceptable. Because I am a creature of habit, I continued to go there, even when my friends began to say that the cappuccino really wasn't all that good. But by then I knew the women behind the counter, was on familiar terms with the owner, often bumped into friends there, exchanged pleasantries every morning with Mille, the Bosnian beggar who sat at the bottom of the bridge leading to the hospital.

Occasionally, if I found myself in some other part of the city, I'd have a cappuccino, and they always tasted better, especially at Gobetti, but I hardly wanted to walk all the way to Ponte dei Pugni every morning just for a cappuccino, did I? There was Tonolo, but that was equally far away. Besides, it was convenient for my best friend Roberta to come and ring my doorbell on her way to work every morning and then continue straight on to Didovich. If I changed, who would ask Mille about his new granddaughter or stop to look at the photos?

Then, in the course of two months, Mille disappeared, and three of the women behind the counter in Didovich quit. One morning, the new woman asked me if I wanted powdered cocoa on top of my cappuccino. What was this, Starbucks?

I informed Roberta, and the next morning we started in search of a new bar. Milani on Strada Nuova had changed hands and the coffee wasn't much good any more; Brasilia hadn't been the same since the old owners sold it about three years earlier. There were the increasing number of Chinese bars, but I assumed that if the food in the Chinese restaurants was consistently bad, and they've had a couple of thousand years to work on that, then they were not to be trusted with cappuccino, were they? Rosa Salva in Campo San Giovanni e Paolo was too far, and I hardly wanted to walk Roberta all the way to work in Campo San Maurizio so that we could stop in the ex-Háagen-Dazs in Campo San Stefano, where the coffee was excellent and the pastries came from Gobetti, though the brioche were those frozen ones that get heated up.

The bar around the corner used UHT milk, and the one just at the back of the Miracoli, though it had Illy coffee, had those same frozen brioche. The unthinkable loomed: breakfast at home.

But then the clouds parted, and we rediscovered Ballarin. One could carbon-date the length of time people have lived in Venice by what they call Ballarin. It had had that name for about four years, and before that it was Zanon and before that Marchini, so to some people it was ex-Zanon and to others ex-Marchini. Many revealed their newness in the city by referring to it as Ballarin. It was just down the street from COIN, opposite Rizzo, and had wonderful pastries and excellent cappuccino. It was very small, always crowded, the service polite and very fast, and there was, mercifully, no danger of cocoa.

17. Wagner

A girl simply never knows what's going to happen on any given day. This is certainly sufficient inducement to get a person out of bed and into the stream of humanity and the new experiences that the day is likely to offer. So it was some years ago, on the day before St Valentine's, when a glorious, sunny day in Venice lured me from my work and out into the streets to go for a walk and see what adventures were to be found.

Because it had been wet and cold for some days, the streets were busy with other people who had chosen to escape confinement to say hello to the sun. San Marco seemed a sensible place to go because, after checking to see that the Basilica was still there, I could go down to Campo Santo Stefano and have a coffee.

In Via XXII Marzo, I stopped to look in a shop window, when I heard a man's voice ask, from behind me, 'Excuse me, are you Donna Leon?'

I turned and saw a handsome man about my own age, wearing a very good suit and tie, a dark overcoat draped over his shoulders, standing a half metre from me. I said that I was, and he gave me a smile so warm and friendly that I had no choice but to return it.

He had a long-stemmed red rose in his right hand, and so I said, hoping to break the awkward silence that results when one party in a conversation does not know the other, 'Ah, you've come to visit Venice?'

He nodded, and that encouraged me to ask, 'Are you coming to visit your *fidanzata*?'

This question appeared to confuse him, so I said, pointing, 'The rose.'

He looked down at it, as though he was seeing it for the first time, and said, 'Oh, no, not for that.'

I was somewhat at a loss because there are not a lot of other reasons for a man to be walking through the streets of Venice with a single red rose in his hands.

'Ah, you're not?' I asked, hoping I had not somehow asked an embarrassing question.

'No,' he said, his face growing softer, and more handsome, as he spoke. 'It's for The Master.'

I smiled in return and looked around to assure myself that I was in a public place, with many people passing by, and therefore probably safe.

'Ah, The Master,' I repeated, taking a small step backwards. I remembered thinking that the door to La Coupole had been open when I passed it, so I could quickly duck into the shop if he made a sudden move.

'Yes, he died today,' he explained. 'I come every year to lay a flower on the steps of the Casinò.' I was about to take another step backwards when the clouds parted and the sun swept down on both of us.

'Ah, *that* Master,' I said, it no longer necessary that I be in a safe place. 'Where he died.'

'Yes,' he said, and a cloud of sadness passed across his face.

'And why is that?' I enquired politely.

'I'm the President of the International Wagner Society,' he explained, suddenly shifting the rose to his left hand and extending his right.

I shook it gladly, pleased to meet a person who had the courage of his passions and who loved the music, and its creator, so much as to make this gesture. 'It's not a painful experience, is it?' I wanted to know.

'No,' he said, shaking the idea away. 'Because there's the music.'

Indeed, I thought, there is the music, isn't there? 'How very good of you,' I said, making no attempt to disguise my admiration.

'Do you love opera?' he asked.

'Oh, yes. I do.' And then I decided that one enthusiast should be honest with another and added, 'It's my greatest joy.'

Understandably, he took this to mean that I felt this way for the sort of opera he felt this way about and he burst out, 'Oh, would you like to come to the Festival?'

My thoughts fled to my best and oldest friend, Peggy, who was a mad Wagnerian, loved the operas, went to see them regularly, and who had, for at least a decade, been on the waiting list for Bayreuth. With no success. We had been friends since high school, I'd been witness at her wedding, she was as close to being my sister as anyone had ever come.

'Ah, the Festival,' I repeated.

'Yes, if you'd like to come, it would be my pleasure to offer you two tickets.'

Peggy had helped me cheat on my final exam in chemistry by passing me the notes she was using to cheat her way through it, thus assuring that we both graduated from high school. Peggy had gone to visit my parents once a week during my first extended stay in Europe. I had what was pretty much my own room in their New York apartment.

'Ah,' I said, putting on a sad face, 'I'm terribly sorry, but I'll be in the States during the entire Festival this year. But it would be very kind if you'd give me your card. Perhaps another year.'

He presented me his card, which I still have in a Fortnum & Mason tea box where I keep business cards. He glanced at his watch and said he had to get the next boat to the Casinò because he was going back to Germany that evening.

We shook hands, two opera lovers meeting by chance on a street to speak of the Master and of what was perhaps our equal passion for the art. After that, he went his way and I continued on my own.

18. *Caigo*

Some years ago, I was on my way home through a fog-blinded Venice. I'd not seen fog that thick for decades: this was *caigo*. It was dense, almost palpable, blinding. The world was white, and everything beyond a distance of a metre had been obliterated. Familiar buildings and bridges had to be read in Braille; I came down the bridge and started across Campo Santa Maria Formosa, my hand on the walls to keep track of where I was. Forms appeared from the fog, everyone's speed reduced to a crawl, all of us blind.

I was somewhere in the middle of the *campo*, more alone than I'd ever been in my life, when suddenly from my right I heard the angels singing 'Hallelujah.' (This is true: I swear it on the head of my mother.)

I forgot how to walk and stopped in place. Yes, it was a choir, singing what is perhaps the most famous musical cliché ever written, and although their voices had to fight their way through the fog, it had to be Handel, and it had to be the Hallelujah chorus.

I shuffled my way to the right, then to the left and saw light fighting its way from the door of the church of Santa Maria Formosa. Silence came with it. And then an ethereal soprano voice told me, *'I know that my Redeemer liveth,'* and my faith was confirmed. I'd stumbled upon a performance of *Messiah*: in the fashion of Venice, there had been no posters, no information, no announcement, and Part III had begun.

I slipped through the door as an usher was closing it and stood, fully open to the power of this music.

'I know that my Redeemer liveth,' the soprano told me. Well, all right; I know it, too.

'The trumpet shall sound,' the bass declared. And why should it not?

'O death, where is thy sting? O grave, where is thy victory?' the alto and tenor enquired of one another. Certainly not here, never with this music.

'Worthy is the Lamb,' the chorus asserted. Indeed.

And then it rushed over us, that four-minute choral 'Amen', as if all of us were being told to stand and affirm that every word we'd just heard was the Truth. And why was it not? Every note of the music was.

In that instant, in tears, as happens every time I listen to *Messiah*, I was willing to toss away a lifetime of non-belief and accept the truth of what had just been sung to us.

19. Sir Peter Jonas

It is lamentably seldom these days that the formation of a friendship can be attributed to a dinosaur, but this was indeed the case with my friendship with Peter Jonas. A quarter of a century ago – just think – I saw the revelatory production of Handel's *Giulio Cesare* at the Bayerische Staatsoper in Munich – of which the dinosaur was a part – and some days later, when I was at least partially recovered from the experience, I wrote – as my great-aunt Gert had instructed all members of my family – a thank-you note to the person responsible, Peter Jonas.

Some weeks later, I received a response – handwritten – from Peter, the intendant and thus the person responsible, who invited me to come along and see another performance when next I was in Munich, and to stop in and say hello.

It is perhaps just as rare as a dinosaur on stage that one's first meeting with someone who will become a friend is delayed because the person to be met is busy standing on his head. But it was the lunch break when I went to visit, and I was told that Peter was in the habit of spending that time on his head. When Peter returned to his feet, I went into his office, and there began the many chats and the friendship.

The link between us was, assuredly, our shared passion for the music of Handel, though his addiction was far more advanced and far more important. After all, he used – praise the Lord – his position to change the listening habits of a continent.

Before Peter put that towering dinosaur on the stage, Handel was presented in a few European festivals in a style akin to Birkenstocks worn with socks. Thump, thump, bump, a hundred voices singing the Hallelujah chorus, and Cesare sung by a bass. Post-dinosaur and for his entire tenure as intendant, the Staatsoper became the most famous opera house in Europe, and Handel won back his place as the leading opera composer of the day.

Today, Handel is everywhere, and he's there because of Peter and the genius of those first productions, when he pretty much grabbed the opera-going public of a continent by the ears and demanded, as Hamlet did of Gertrude, 'How like you this ... ?' A great deal, as it turned out, and praise Peter for that, always.

I was struck at the beginning by three qualities I saw in him and that remained intact at our last meeting: intelligence, decency, and charm. He was smart, and his knowledge and understanding swept from music to history, economics, science and astronomy, and then back to art. He was not in the business of making moral judgements, though he had an ethical sense that disapproved of cheating and valued civility. Even with this, he never conquered his childlike wonderment at the many ways in which adults could misbehave. And he had charm. My God, the man could charm a statue from its plinth.

Over the years, then the decades, we met occasionally, corresponded intermittently, but – no matter how long the gap had been – we always picked up the conversation where it had stopped.

Peter was Scheherazade, truth to tell. Because of the marvelous variety of his studies, travels, work, and friendships, there was always something or someone he could pick out of his memory, and there were certain stories I'd ask him to tell me again and again. I confess I had many favorites and made specific requests to hear them.

One favorite was his visit in Jamaica to his incarcerated cousins, busy running the island's drug business from the suites they maintained – with private, uniformed, and heavily armed guards – inside the prison where they were being held, one of the few places where they were safe.

Another was the story of a soprano, whose name he never revealed, who came into his office in a raincoat, locking the door behind her. She had come to request that he allow her to cancel her contract so that she could accept a better one in another country. When he refused, she untied her raincoat (think Ingrid Bergman in *Casablanca*), under which she wore nothing, and said she'd do anything if he'd agree. The best part of the story was his acting out of his fumbling grab for the telephone, begging his secretary to come into the office immediately and save him.

He also spoke of his schooldays in the fifties at a Benedictine boys' school, which he described as a gulag with a crucifix in every room. What always touched me most about his telling of the story was his nostalgia for these boys, caught at the age of first lust and with only confused ideas about what to do with it.

In all of his stories, Peter presented himself as a bumbling innocent, not at all sure what to think or do: the tone was pure slapstick, and judgement was never dragged into the telling of the tale.

Alas, there were also stories of the enemy who walked just one step behind him for most of his life: cancer. He once told me how many times he'd been diagnosed and how many operations he'd had. It would be normal, here, to write 'that he endured', but he spoke of his medical history only with scientific interest and distance and thus spared the hearer the pain of understanding. I remember his description of the enormous cannon, many metres long, that was going to shoot a single atom into his eye, for he had so often outwitted his cancers that his eye was one of the few places left for it to attack. His real curiosity about the process was so contagious – I suspect this was Peter's desire – that the listener, too, became so intrigued by the mystery and complexity of the treat-ment as to be diverted from the fact that this was a deadly disease making yet another attack on a beloved friend.

Our last meeting was meant to be the first of a lark-ish plan we had to record him talking about his life, and then we'd somehow turn it into his autobiography. We chatted, we had lunch, more chat, and then the story of his cousins for dessert, coffee, and then off I went, delighted with the stories and his intelligence and company as well as with his thoughtfulness in having had coffee ice cream for us both. And planning to continue it the next time we were in the same city at the same time.

That never happened, and now he's gone. But his memory stays: he was the best storyteller I ever knew, my life was immeasurably enriched by his friendship, and I've never met a man who looked better wearing a kilt.

20. Von Clausewitz at Rialto

I'm a peaceful person. However, like many of my sort, I take a keen interest in observing the behaviour – one might even say the tactics – of those people who are not. Human aggression, no matter how we attempt to suppress it, will slip from whatever restraint is placed upon it, and all high notions regarding human behaviour will crumble in the face of the desire to expand and possess. This was a reality well understood by Carl von Clausewitz, the Prussian general whose *On War* is one of the classic texts on the subject.

This book might seem an odd place for the General to make an appearance, were it not for my conviction that his text is much favored by Venetian women of a certain age. Perhaps they turn to it when the last grandchild is born, or when they finally stop dyeing their hair, or simply when they decide that, since there are not many more years left, they would prefer to live the last ones in the manner of the lion and not the lamb. For what else could explain the remarkably astute tactics common to the old women who do their grocery shopping at the Rialto Market?

Von Clausewitz took Napoleon – audacious, aggressive, careless of human life – as his example when he wrote about warfare, which the Prussian viewed as an inseparable part of normal political life. Diplomacy and negotiation came first, von Clausewitz argued, and only when both failed was one obliged to resort to warfare; once begun, war was to be absolute and merciless. Ah, how very like the behaviour of the women in the midst of whom I did my grocery shopping for decades, though most of them seem to have overlooked the General's remarks about diplomacy and negotiation.

Let us begin with von Clausewitz's definition of war: 'War therefore is an act of violence intended to compel our opponent to fulfil our will.' The overriding desire of the aggression displayed by the old women at Rialto is, indeed, to compel the opponent to fulfil their will, namely that they be served the instant they arrive, regardless of how many people are already in line. The opponent is any other customer, and the act of violence is usually committed not against those people but against the established rule of taking one's turn in the order in which people arrive at the counter.

'The compulsory submission of the enemy to our will is the ultimate object.' In order to compel this submission, von Clausewitz continues, 'The number [of troops] will determine victory ... only it must be sufficiently great to be a counterpoise to all the other cooperating circumstances.' Further, he believes that 'the greatest possible number of troops should be brought into action at the decisive point.'

Obviously, a small woman weighing between fifty and fifty-five kilos, standing perhaps 1.5 metres tall, is not likely to bring the greatest number of troops into action in front of the pecorino, is she? Thus she will be forced to fall back on 'cooperating circumstances', which in her case are the traditions deep-rooted in Italian society regarding the deference and respect that must be given to old people, especially old women, and which, well she knows, weaken her opponents sufficiently to render them vulnerable to her attack. Rather than bring up the cavalry at a particular moment, rather than fling the Imperial Guard into a charge in one last attempt at victory, she will use the wily stratagem of Feigned Astonishment. Usually, it works.

This manoeuvre is a simple one and is almost always successful. Its genius lies in its obviousness: surely no person would so brazenly push past six others lined up at the cheese counter unless she had a legitimate reason to do so? Like most unexpected attacks, it must be launched with nonchalance to keep the manoeuvre from being detected for as long as possible. It is important, too, that at this early stage the attacking force avoids all physical contact. She is, after all, a small person and so can insinuate herself between shoulders and hips, avoid knocking over other people's shopping bags, and arrive smack up against the counter, first in line.

Once she is in possession of the territory, she will allow one person to be served ahead of her, the better to tranquillize the opposing forces: 'Stratagem implies a concealed intention, and therefore is opposed to straightforward dealing.' Then, at the question from the cheese seller, '*Chi tocca?*', she will shoot up her hand to indicate that she is next and begin to give her first order. Italians, trained to be respectful (especially to a woman the same age as their grandmothers), will remain mute. The merchant, no doubt long familiar with her tactic, has the option of either questioning her assertion, and thus losing her as a customer, or passively serving her – another 'cooperating circumstance'. Should it happen, however, that her claim is called into question, she will employ the tactic of Feigned Astonishment and ask, 'Oh, were you before me?'

Should her opponent be tempted to answer sharply, perhaps slip into irony or sarcasm, the old woman will summon her forces with breathtaking speed and launch the attack of Bold Denial. 'I didn't see you'; 'I was here first'; 'That man in the green shirt was the only one here when I arrived'; 'All I want is one thing.' Should a person be so rash as to ignore the centuries of training to which the Italians waiting at the counter have been subjected and be tempted to argue with her, that person risks going against von Clausewitz's admonition that 'even if we are decidedly superior in strength, and are able to repay the enemy his victory by a greater still, it is always better to forestall the conclusion of a disadvantageous combat'. Bear in mind that *any* opposition to one of these women constitutes a 'disadvantageous combat', for she will not retreat and she will never surrender: she was there first, and that is the end of it. They know, these old women, that 'there is nothing in war which is of greater importance than obedience', and in Italy people are still obedient to the social rule that dictates patience with the old.

Furthermore, most people doing the grocery shopping are women, and they are usually more obedient to social convention than men.

Sometimes, however, it proves impossible for her to charge to the head of the queue, and she is constrained to call out her order from the flanks: in this case, she employs what the General calls 'those extraordinary mental powers required in a general' and resorts to Bold Denial. Entrenched in her position, she waves off the existence of a queue, insisting that she was there first, indeed is quite exasperated at having been kept waiting so long.

The success of either of these tactics – see Book III, Chapter 7 for what the good General has to say about perseverance – allows for escalation, and she is thus free to begin giving her order, a feinting manoeuvre that distracts from the audacity of her invasion by diverting attention to the supposed poor quality of the merchandise. Inevitably, this will include comments about the prosciutto she bought last time, a fierce admonition that the fat be cut from the speck before it is sliced, abrupt enquiries into the age of the ricotta, and a sharp exhalation of breath indicative of outraged disbelief at any assertion regarding the quality of the mozzarella.

Von Clausewitz understands not only war but the secrets of the human heart: 'Of all the noble feelings which fill the human heart in the exciting tumult of battle, none, we must admit, are so powerful and con-stant as the soul's thirst for honor and renown.' Consider for a moment how little honor and renown are left to these women as they move towards the end of their lives; consider how shrunken are the battlefields where once, in their youth and their prime, they could do combat in search of respect and power. Strength gone, perhaps widowed or living alone, they are forced to use other means to obtain victory. Their 'concealed intention' – at least, they believe it is concealed – is above all a return to their former status, to their former honor and renown.

Whether they are doing battle in front of the salami or cheese or defending their position in front of the fruit and vegetables, this desire to defend their honor will not leave them. They are the only clients – other than tourists, who simply don't know any better – who will dare to lay their hands on the peaches or rip their own bananas from the bunch.

In the course of four decades, both as a combatant and as a neutral observer when at Rialto with friends, I have never known one of these old women to surrender or retreat. Deaf to all protest, and in the face of comment, sarcasm, or abuse, they have all stood firm, facing the enemy head-on: they will have *this* melon and *these* grapes. As words are fired above them, they will pinch the apricots to see that they are firm, break off a leaf of basil to see – to see what? That it is not plastic? They will complain about the freshness of the zucchini, the size of the potatoes, the few tattered leaves on the outside of a head of lettuce. And even as the glances and mutterings of the other customers burst like grenades above their heads, so fierce does their attack remain that most merchants will give in and strip off the offending leaves or reject a peach if its skin is rougher than that of a newborn baby.

And how are we meant to respond, those of us standing in line as they subtly position themselves in front of us? '... for in such dangerous things as war, the errors which proceed from a spirit of benevolence are the worst.' Doomed by our own goodwill and sympathy, we commit these errors of benevolence, year after year, leaving the field of battle to these wrinkled Amazons. As they shove past us, we should bear in mind that these old women have no choice but to obey von Clausewitz's order that 'the victualling of the troops themselves comes first and must be done almost daily'. Obedient to the rule of war themselves, they have no choice but to attempt to banish all enemies and triumph on the field of battle.

And what of us, as we stand in line, in the fullness of our health and vigour? We might be well advised to recall that 'No battle can take place unless by mutual consent.' If we do persist in combat, what do we gain? Three minutes? Perhaps, then, it is better to leave the field of battle to our adversaries and let them be first in line, restored to honor and renown. Let them return to their tents carrying the laurel (or thyme or parsley) of victory, at least for as long as it takes them to buy *due etti di mortadella e un po' di ricotta affumicata.*

21. Gondola

Because gondolas, to any of us who have lived in Venice for decades, are as common as yellow taxis to a New Yorker, we almost cease to notice them, and thus we seldom give them conscious thought. We passively observe that all other boats defer to them and give them right of way, and the shout of the *gondolieri* approaching a turn is part of the background noise of the city. If we use them at all, it is as a convenient *traghetto* service to cross the Grand Canal when we are in a hurry or burdened with produce from the Rialto Market. Thus it was only by force of coincidence that their familiar invisibility entered my conscious mind, aroused my curiosity.

An American friend was given as a Christmas present – I believe it was meant to be a joke – the blueprints of a gondola, complete with detailed instructions. He opened the plans and began to spread them out on the dinner table. As he unfolded the paper, more and more bottles, plates, and cutlery had to be removed to the sideboard or taken back into the kitchen. The paper expanded. When the edges of the blueprint were hanging over the four sides of the table, he turned from them and began to read the instructions that accompanied them.

The other guests at the dinner were forced to balance their plates on their knees or abandon the idea of food altogether and content themselves with wine and conversation. If it is possible to ignore a person looming over a two-metre-long blueprint, muttering to himself, then we ignored him. Until suddenly he said, his face alight with a vision of the finished gondola, 'I think I could do this.'

Another revelation also came at dinner, as is so often the case in Italy, though this was in a different part of the city and with different guests. A friend lives on the Grand Canal, which means glory and beauty and bliss and endless delight. It also means, alas, gondola-loads of tourists back and forth under the windows, and since these are the gondolas working with large groups of tourists, an accordionist and a singer are tossed in. (Oh, how tempting is that phrase.)

As we ate our risotto, we heard the – dare I use this word? – music approaching. The accordionist squeezed out some notes, and the voice of what I had once heard my Irish grandmother call 'a whisky tenor' rose up to the mezzanine apartment and the words of "O sole mio' flew up to scandalize us all.

At that point, the host's dachshund, Artù, leaped up (well, he struggled up because he was a dachshund) onto the wide windowsill, pitched his head back, and began to howl like what that same grandmother would have called a banshee. Beside himself, either with the pain caused by the music – pain that we shared – or perhaps deluding himself that this noise came from his dog pack and he was being called upon to declare his solidarity with them, Artù howled his head off while the boatloads of tourists below snapped photographs and waved up at him. During this, the gondolier, not the tenor, shouted up, 'Ciao, Artù. Che togo che ti xe.' I have many friends who are singers: none of them has ever had a *gondoliere* call up to tell him how very beautiful he is, nor has any one of them been photographed, head back and howling, by boatloads of Japanese tourists.

Let me leave Artù to his art and return my attention to the Master Builder. Construction began not in Venice but about an hour from the city, where my American friend had access to a complete carpenter's workshop with ample space to work on the boat. No, he is not a professional carpenter, though he has for years built cabinets, tables, doors, even an elaborate drop-front writing desk. But not, until then, had he thought of building a gondola. Alone.

A year passed. Every so often, I went to visit him and to have a look at the project, feeling not a little like Peter the Great stopping by to see how the Hermitage was progressing. I spent the best part of one afternoon watching him curve the oak boards that would form the sides of the gondola. This required that they be kept wet on top while he played a blowtorch across them from below as he moulded the eleven-metre planks into the proper shape. The frame took a year, and then he began to insert the *sancón* and the *piàna*, the stabilizing bars that run from side to side of the bottom, which would eventually be covered by the floorboards or *pagiòl*. I realized how much an exercise in three-dimensionality the construction was, for the two sides curve up – as if the boat were a giant lop-sided banana – to encompass a hollow space, and the builder must continually calculate just what is next and where it goes in relation to the other pieces.

As another year passed, the area covered by his project expanded, until one room of the carpenter's workshop was filled with lengths of wood, rectangles of wood, rods and strips and pegs and pieces for which there is no English – and no Italian – name. Not only had a large section of the workshop been turned into *uno squero*, but one of his workbenches was now home to scores of oddly shaped pieces of wood. Stranger still, the Italian carpenter often asked the American to explain to him the details of cutting and planing the *nómbolo* (side planks), *pirón* (wooden bolts and nails), and *pontapìe* (inclined wooden brace for the *gondoliere*'s back foot). As to the *trèsso*, the carpenter's uncertainty might result from this definition given to it: *'listelli fissati sull'orlo interno di alcuni sancóni per sostenere rispettivamente il sentàr, le banchéte e il tristolìn da próva inferiore'*. Obviously, these are instructions that make sense only to a Venetian gondola builder. Eventually, the carpenter was to observe the creation of more than two hundred structural and semi-structural, functional and non-functional parts, including a large number of simple wooden planks. Here I should add that the gondola, unlike the jigsaw puzzle, does not come with ready-cut pieces. The person – though it is virtually unheard of for a single person to attempt it – building the boat has to cut each piece by hand or machine and shape it so precisely that it fits smoothly into the pieces around it. Watertight, remember?

Another year passed, and my friend arrived at the *trasto de mèso* and began thinking about where to find the most beautiful *fórcola*, upon which the oar is braced, though I had learned enough by then to realize there was going to be no need of a *fórcola* for some time yet, at least a year. The *fórcola* can't be slipped into place until the entire boat is completed, but I chose to interpret his interest as optimism, not magical thinking. As the boat grew, the room began to clear: less space was taken up by unused pieces, just as the closer one comes to completing a puzzle, the fewer pieces lie loose on the table.

Towards the beginning of the fourth year, he reached the point of constructing the *parti decorative*, the *sentolìna* and the *caenèla*. By then, the carpenter had been transformed from a rent-collecting Saul to a Saint Paul, fully converted and eager to participate, although my friend allowed him to help only with heavy lifting, never with the actual work of construction.

When the frame was complete, it was necessary to caulk, which is done with thin strings of cotton that must be soaked in resin and then wedged into the tiny grooves between the interlocking boards from which the boat is built. These strings are sealed in place with repeated coats of resin; later, before it's painted, pitch will be used to seal the complete interior of the gondola.

While he's busy sealing up the boat to make sure it's watertight, let's go back to Artù, the Fritz Wunderlich of Palazzo Curti Valmarana. Through the days and evenings of a hot summer, the tourists floated by, the accordionist played, and Artù conquered. An American movie producer, hearing Artù in concert, talked of the possibility of his appearing in a cameo role in a new film version of *Romeo e Giulietta*. Even though we knew that the words of American film producers are as permanent as those written on the waters of the Grand Canal, a few of us permitted ourselves an evening discussing costumes and shooting angles. I remember one heated discussion of whether Artù's right profile was better than his left and from which side, therefore, to film him. I'm afraid I grew quite severe here and suggested that, should negotiations ever lead to this point, the only place from which to shoot Artù was the floor.

Time passed, his owner did not hear from the producer, and finally the film was made without Artù's artistic contribution. He, however, continued to sing. As the months went by and I heard the repertory of the human singers time after time, I realized that the two most often-sung songs that waft their way up and down the waters of the Grand Canal are those Neapolitan classics 'Torna a Surriento' and "O Sole Mio'. Was a Venetian dog meant to sing along to these? Where, I wondered, was the Venetian music that was really meant to be sung from the gondolas?

By the middle of the fifth year, the gondola was caulked, coated with countless layers of resin, painted, and judged to be watertight. All of the decorative parts were in place, the *fórcola* bought, and two metal *ferri* attached at front and back. It was time to launch the gondola. To do this, it was necessary to find enough strong men to take it from where it rested in the wooden cradle in the carpenter's workshop and carry it first to a truck. Thirty-two men answered the casting call, a panoply of muscles such as life seldom presents us. They lifted the gondola, all 350 kilos of it, and carried it slowly towards an eight-wheeled heavy transport truck. The driver lowered the winch and then lifted the boat into place on the cradle where it would rest until it reached its destination.

The trip took an hour. I followed behind in a friend's car and thus could see the heads of drivers and passengers whip round as the truck passed them. A gondola? On the autostrada?

In Tronchetto, the parking lot at the end of the bridge from the mainland, another winch cradled the gondola and lifted it from the truck, then lowered it gently into the water. As soon as they heard the story, the people in the growing crowd at the dock lined up on the edge, waiting to see if it would sink or swim.

It swam, and the heroic builder finally climbed down into his boat, walked to the back, and took the oar that a friend handed down to him. In jeans and tennis shoes, without a straw hat, and with no Neapolitan singer at midship, he started to row away from the dock, heading towards the entrance to the Grand Canal.

Those of us who had come along with him to Venice to watch the launch started to cheer, and soon we were joined by the workers on the pier. Our shouts and whistles must have created a strong wind or current behind him, for very soon he disappeared into the darkness under the railway bridge. Then, a few long minutes later, he appeared again in the sunlight on the other side, turned in an arc to the right, and disappeared into the beginning of the Grand Canal. This time, it was the assembled dock workers and boatmen who started to cheer, and soon we were all standing there, pounding one another on the shoulder, cheering at the boat that was finally on its way home.

22. Waiting for the Plumber

All right: confess. How much time, during your entire life, have you spent waiting for the plumber? Hours? Days? Can we all agree that the most necessary person, at least when there is need to arrive at a home disaster quickly, is the plumber. A person can get on with candles for a day or so, iPhones have a flashlight, and most people know where the fuse box is. But how many of us know where to find the central control (I don't even know the right word) that lets the water into the house, or even knows where to find the tap that turns off the water to the kitchen?

That's a worst-case scenario. Luckily, every visit from the plumber is not necessarily an exercise in disaster prevention. Plumbers can also, at least in Italy, inspect and certify a building's heating system for the amount of pollution it produces, confirming that the burner presents no risk to the residents of the building or to the environment.

Some years ago, I called my Rastafarian (yes) plumber and asked if he were authorized to inspect my water heater and issue the necessary government document stating that everything was in order.

'No, Signora,' he said. 'You need to call a *termotecnico* for that.' When asked for clarification as to the difference between himself and a *termotecnico*, he paused a moment before explaining that it was much like the difference between an MRI machine and open-heart surgery. The *termotecnico* discovered; someone else fixed.

Still faintly uneasy at the comparison he had made, I asked if he knew someone reliable. His brother-in-law, as it turned out, was a *termotecnico* and yes, he did have his phone number. It took me three calls before I spoke to Alessandro, who said he would be able to come at the end of the following week. I accepted, thankful that he was not a mere plumber coming to turn off the water flooding across my kitchen floor from a broken pipe.

Alessandro had to change the date and time twice, but in both cases it was for '*un emergenza*'. When the day arrived, he was smack on time for our appointment and announced himself over the speakerphone as 'Alessandro.' I pressed the door release and told him, 'Third floor.'

After a moment, I opened the door at the top of the steps and listened to his footsteps, trying to estimate his age. They were very quiet footsteps at normal speed, sixty-seven of them. After a short time, a man

appeared at the bottom of the last flight, and I con-
cluded that this was the wrong Alessandro, for I was
awaiting the arrival of a man in much-worn jeans,
wearing construction boots with metal protection on
the toes, dressed in a too-large padded jacket. And
because of his relationship to my own plumber, perhaps a woollen cap into which were stuffed his many
braids.

But, no, Alessandro, a man in his early thirties with
professionally tousled golden hair and a profile I'd last
seen on coins dating to the epoch of the Emperor
Heliogabalus, wore a beige zippered jacket that had
surely been made of the skins of some endangered
species of goat native to the Pamir Mountains. His
jeans, I'm sure, had been stitched by Giorgio Armani
himself, and his shoes, a pair of Santoni tasselled loaf-
ers, probably cost more than my water heater.

Alessandro carried a thin leather briefcase (no han-
dle; it would ruin the line), from which he pulled an
equally thin apparatus that closely resembled a computer, but wasn't. He set it gently on the kitchen
counter. Did he have a toolkit? A screwdriver? Not a
bit of it. Only some thin black cables that he proceeded
to remove from the briefcase. When all of these things
were arrayed on the counter to the left of the heater, he
unzipped his jacket. I asked him for it, went back to
the bedroom and found a padded coat hanger and
slipped its arms gently into the jacket, careful not to
rub the end of the coat hanger against the grain of the
leather.

I hung it in the closet, hoping this would assure
Alessandro that I would be patience itself until he

entered my name alongside all the rule-observing Venetians. When I turned back to him, he had opened the computer-that-wasn't and attached two wires to slots on its right side.

I noticed then that he had removed the lower cover of the heater, exposing its viscera. He attached the cables to two tiny sockets and began to type furiously into the computer-that-wasn't.

He would occasionally pause, watching the screen with severe attention. Occasionally, we'd both hear the heater flame into function, then lower itself and stop, only to resume instantly with a greater roar. Each time the flame roared, he typed in new information, paused for the response, nodded, gave more information, pursed his lips, and entered more information. All that existed for him was the keyboard, the screen, and his furious typing.

Some time later, he stopped, seemingly exhausted, and raised his hands slowly, and I thought of Angela Hewitt gently raising hers from the keyboard after playing the *Goldberg Variations*.

He closed the cover of the computer-that-wasn't and slid it into the briefcase, then freed the cables at both ends and slipped them in beside it. He allowed the rapture to fade and smiled. 'Would you like me to mail a bill?' he asked, using the same tone that some parents use when asking, 'Do I have to tell you that again?'

'Oh, no. Perhaps I could pay you in cash?'

'Ah, yes. That might be possible,' he said, as though the idea had never crossed his mind.

'And how much would that be?'

'That depends.'

'On what?'

'On whether you'd ask for a receipt or not.'

'If I do?'

'One hundred and twenty.'

'And if I don't?'

'Ninety.'

I saw myself then as the person who would help Alessandro acquire his next pair of shoes, perhaps something comfortable from Bottega Veneta, although I accepted my humble position and knew I'd be paying for little more than the lambskin tassels.

'I think I don't need a receipt, Signor Alessandro,' I said, happy to do my own small part in maintaining this pillar of Italian culture.

23. Cruise Ships

Last week, I stopped by to visit a friend who has an apartment on the Riva della Giudecca, from the living room of which four large windows look back towards San Marco. Occasionally, I've gone there for the feast of the Redentore, stood at those windows and watched the fireworks blaze up from the rafts in the Bacino, seen them fire up the sky and illuminate the most beautiful urban space in the world.

I thought I was there for a coffee, but things suddenly got very interesting when he said, after I finished my coffee, 'Come into the bedroom.' Now, he was thirty years younger than I, I'd cried at his wedding not a month before, and his wife was sitting with us at the table, so perhaps this offer was a bit different from what it at first appeared to be.

Docile, wondering what on earth was afoot, I followed him into the room. 'Sit on the bed,' he said, pointing to a spot on the far side, facing the window that looked out to the north side of the island.

I did as I was told and sat. 'Look at this,' he said, placing a finger on the wall and running it down what I now perceived to be a line in the paint. More than a line. Was that, could that be, was this possibly...? Indeed, a long vertical crack that started halfway up the wall and ran down to the floor.

Though I lived in Venice for more than twenty-five years and spent at least fifty of them listening to people talk about real estate, I can never remember if the bad cracks are the ones that go up and down or the ones that go from side to side. 'Look closer,' he said, switching off the bedroom light, and again I did as I was told. Coming into the room from the outside was a thin line of light, which meant that the crack was not in the paint, not in the stucco behind it, and not in the first line of bricks, but was a crack that tore open the fabric of the building.

We went back to the living room, and I went back to the contemplation of the Bell Tower of San Marco, off in the distance. We discussed the crack. An hour later, after our conversation had drifted off to other things, I heard a low grumbling noise from my left, a noise so loud as to pull me up from my chair.

After a few minutes, the Bell Tower, the Basilica, indeed, the entire opposite side of the canal disappeared, to be replaced by a seven-storey cruise ship, preceded by a jolly tugboat, as it sailed away from the city, its happy thousands having had their chance to have a day or perhaps even a day and a half in Venice.

On the table, the water in my glass trembled; indeed, the table itself was trembling when I placed my hand upon it. The passing ship filled me with a faint unease, just as it filled my friend with a despair that was not at all faint.

For years, the various, and ever more numerous, cruise ships have brought their thousands to the city: on any given day, there can be two, three, four of them moored down in San Basilio, their little duck lines of tourists streaming down the gangplanks to go off after their umbrella-carrying guides. In their hours in the city, they discover the beauty of La Serenissima, the city-state that once ruled the seas. Perhaps they shop. Perhaps they buy a sandwich or a coffee. They have very little time to spend in the city.

An article in my Bible, the *Gazzettino*, reported that these ships, in order to continue to provide air conditioning, heat, hot water, electricity, plumbing for the thousands of people on board, must keep their motors running while they are in port, and that each of these ships thus produces the same exhaust as 14,000 cars left parked at the docks with their motors running. As with any statistic produced here, there is no way to know its exact relationship with the truth. Even a tenth of that number would be bad enough: remember that the number refers to each of the two, three, four ships.

Every Venetian who talks to me laments the presence, and the constant passage, of these ships. Every year the people living anywhere within striking distance of the Giudecca Canal are forced to sit helpless, month by month and year by year, as their buildings and churches, even the back walls of their bedrooms, are shaken and sundered to the ground. The presence of these ships brings some financial gain to the city, for the passengers do manage to buy this and that, graze among the *pizzerie* and sandwich stalls of the city, before going back to eat and sleep on board.

The city administration wrings its hands at the signs of damage, as do the people whose homes are being shaken down. But there are multiple government agencies in charge of the waters around Venice, and so any decision must be made by and among them. Until they decide what to do, the boats will sail up and down, and the crack on the back wall of my friend's bedroom will grow wider and wider.

Bon voyage!

24. Letter for the Questore

This letter, in both English and German, is currently being given to tourists who go to the Questura at Campo San Lorenzo in search of Commissario Brunetti. It was written at the request of the Questore, Dottor Maurizio Masciopinto, who asked me to write something to convince the visitors that Dottor Brunetti is not in the employ of the Polizia di Stato and thus cannot be found at the Questura.

Dear Reader,
  Welcome to the Questura of Venice! Your enthusiasm for Commissario Brunetti and the people who work with and for him has brought you here, after having walked and gotten lost in the streets of Venice. If you were looking for Brunetti,

or Signorina Elettra, Vianello, even for Vice-Questore Patta, I have to tell you, much to my regret, that they are not here today but are on a training course outside the city. However, you can still see the church of San Lorenzo, the canal, the dock for the police launch, and Palazzo Ziani, the building that houses the real police as well as those in the books.

The characters in the books are, of course, fictional. The people working inside the Questura – and I have known some of them for years – are far more serious about and far better at their work than are some of the characters in the books. In fact, the real police do an excellent job of keeping the city safe, and it remains one of the safest cities in the world.

When the characters return from their course, they will go back to being what they are. Alvise will continue to make a fool of himself, Rizzardi will give his respectful attention to the dead, Vianello will still know almost everyone in the city, and Griffoni will continue to suffer in her small office.

And Signorina Elettra? I confess that I have no idea at all of what she is doing or how she does it. I know only that she does it with her computer and with the contacts she has with people who know things she wants to know. And she wears wonderful clothing.

Brunetti will continue to read the Greek and Roman classics in the hope that these writers will help him understand the nature of justice.

I'd like to thank you for the enthusiasm that has led you to the Questura and hope that future books will continue to interest and please you.

Most sincerely,
Donna Leon

Part Four:
In the Mountains

25. Other Countries, Other Habits

I've been spending so much time in Switzerland in recent years that I fear living there has corrupted me. If trains are late, I grumble; if the plumber comes fifteen minutes late, I am shocked. Corrupted, you see.

Recently, in Venice for a week, I had reason to go to the post office to mail two letters: one to France and one to England; the French letter had six pages and thus was heavier than a normal letter.

I went happily along to the main post office near Rialto and – efficiency being the new rallying cry of the Ufficio Postale – took my number from the machine, the same kind one finds in large bakeries or the cheese counter of a supermarket: P64. Well, P46 was being served; one did not need much mathematical skill to conclude that this was going to be a long wait.

Inspired by what a friend had told me about another post office that had recently opened, and cheered by the fact that it was a glorious autumn day, I decided to spend ten minutes walking through the most beautiful city in the world to go mail my letters in a smaller post office.

This post office is a bit of a secret: those who use it do not tell people about it, nor, I suspect, do the people who work there. Always keep a good thing to yourself. When I arrived (and, like everyone else, I will *not* tell you where it is), there was no number machine and only two people in line in front of me. I took my place and within a minute was standing at the counter. A moment later, a friend came in and stood in line behind me.

I presented my two letters and said I wanted to mail them, as if there were any other reason to carry letters to a post office. The man behind the counter smiled, took them, and put the first one on his scale. He hit a few keys on his computer. Nothing happened, so he removed the letter, shook it a bit, and placed it on the scale again. He gave a command to the computer. A short time passed, after which the printer growled and spat out a piece of sticky paper the size of a granola bar; on it was printed a single stamp.

The postman took the paper and, seeing that it was too big to fit in the top right of the envelope, wrapped it around the bottom right and placed it carefully on the counter in front of him.

He took the second letter and repeated the process, having to remove it once from the scale so that the computer could not only resuscitate itself but also recalculate the letter's weight and the price of the stamp. Again, the two-dimensional granola bar slid out of the machine, and he attached it to the same place on the envelope.

He looked up and smiled, evidently pleased with his work, and asked if I'd like anything else. How much does a letter sent within Europe cost? One euro. Could I buy twenty stamps, perhaps? Then I don't have to bother you every time I send a letter.

'I'm sorry, Signora, but I don't have any stamps.'

I glanced at the woman to his left and asked if the postman could perhaps buy some for me from his colleague, who was busy selling stamps to another client. He could not have been more delighted by the idea and all but fell from his chair as he leaned towards her and asked for twenty one-euro stamps.

He counted the stamps, touching each one as he did so, as though he wanted to be sure they were firmly attached to the sticky paper. I watched his finger move across the stamps, although that verb is perhaps too active for what he was doing.

He gave me the stamps, and I gave him thirty euros. He entered the cost of the two letters and the stamps on his computer, which calculated the same sum I had. His smile came along with the change, and I glanced at my watch, idly curious to know how long this had all taken. Seven minutes. To mail two letters and buy some stamps.

I smiled and turned to leave and, at the door, met another friend. 'If I were to tell my friends how long this took, they'd be amazed,' I said, thinking that, in Zurich, it might have taken a minute to send two letters and buy twenty stamps. Realizing that my friend was Italian, I regretted my words and the offence they were sure to give: don't spit in the plate out of which you eat. Keep your fat mouth shut, please.

No doubt pleased that a foreigner would share her opinion, she smiled and said, 'Yes, they're very fast here, aren't they?'

26. Gotthard

Every profession leads to deformation, I suppose: mine is crime. Ever since I started writing crime fiction, my mind has taken a certain path, like a morning glory seeking the light or a pumpkin vine growing up and over the compost heap. I'm drawn to crime. That is, my imagination tends to criminalize even the most innocent of situations and see them in terms of the sort of crime they might produce or how a greedy or violent person might turn them to his advantage. If I go into a shop to buy a bottle of wine, I might buy a few bottles of prosecco, but my imagination always emerges with a few bottles of Tignanello or Gaja stuffed into my boots or the sleeves of my jacket. I don't know how many cashmere sweaters I've tried on in various shops in this city, always planning how to layer them, one on top of the other, before I slice off the price tags, put my jacket back on, and make a quiet exit from the store. And there is not a pen or notebook I have not secretly slipped from the shelves of Testolini, the stationery store.

Shops are not my only victims: many are the purses I've taken from shopping carts left carelessly in front of the cat food in Billa, the pockets I've picked on a crowded vaporetto, and some time ago, in the church of St George in Hanover Square in London, I could not take my eyes from the wallet left carelessly lying just inside an open purse by a woman who had left her pew to go to Communion.

So I leave it to you to think of what my imagination gets up to as the train approaches the Gotthard Tunnel, whether from the north or from the south. On the way up, we've already had the customs inspection, which means I have to keep my eye on the elegant woman who got on at Como, for I am sure she's got more in that suitcase than a change of clothing. And the guy with the bad haircut: I know he's got large packages of something – drugs, diamonds, plastique – taped to his body. And why did the customs inspector not ask to see the passport of the man who had become increasingly nervous as the train approached the border?

On the trip back to Italy, all of the other passengers are, of course, carrying vast amounts of cash, though I can never figure out just what it is they intend to do with all this money. Buy guns? Buy girls? Buy politicians?

My own smuggling, and this I confess openly, is confined to two products: *parmigiano* on the way north and chocolate on the way south. This way, too, should the train ever become trapped in the Gotthard, I am well prepared to become the new best friend of everyone in the carriage, for on each trip I carry enough with me to maintain the Seventh Fleet for at least one week.

The train trip back and forth between Venice and Zurich is something I actually look forward to. It is, each way, eight hours during which there will be no phone, no fax, no emails. There will be only the chance to sit and read, interrupted by nothing but my own imagination. And interrupt me it does. I don't go to the cinema, so I've no knowledge of disaster films, though I do read about the cinema, and thus am familiar with the burning buildings, the sinking ships, the giant crabs that will inherit the earth after some sort of nuclear disaster. I've read enough disaster books to have become familiar with the formula: whenever disaster can occur, it will. There is always something nasty lurking in the woodshed. Or the tunnel.

Thus, ten kilometres before Airolo, I begin to study the people in the train with me, wondering how they will behave when the inevitable happens: the train enters the long tunnel and, just at midpoint, something happens that will block the tracks both forward and back. Who will be the hero, who the coward, and who the villain? How long will we be trapped? That question inevitably leads my thoughts to the water supply: in all these years of riding European trains, I've always wondered if the 'acqua' really is 'non potabile'. How long will the crackers and panini in the bar hold out? Will there be light? Could I bring myself to drink a Coke? Won't the *parmigiano* make us all terribly thirsty?

Because I don't like to read in the tunnel, I keep my eyes on the protagonists of the drama I am busily constructing. Unlike heroes, cowards, and villains, they have always remained calmly in their seats, reading or talking or sleeping and seemingly entirely unaware of the dramatic futures I am painting for them.

And each time, usually about halfway through the tunnel, I am forced to abandon my fantasy and accept the fact that no train I've been on, in all these years commuting between Venice and Zurich, has ever so much as slowed down in the tunnel. So much for giant crabs. Specific incidents from various trips remain. A few years ago, I made the trip to Zurich on Ferragosto, the day of the grand vacation exodus, when Italians vanish from the country, heading north. The radio had made mention, days before, of the number of cars estimated to be on the roads that weekend, but because I knew I'd be on the train, I'd paid no attention to how many tens of millions it was going to be. But then, as the train got to within a few kilometres of the tunnel, I glanced idly to the right, to the autostrada running parallel to the tracks, and I saw what looked, really, like a scene from one of those disaster films: kilometre after kilometre of stopped cars. People paced around them, many cars had their hoods raised, a few had steam vents erupting from their radiators. The scene lacked only – yes – the giant crab to pull itself up and out of the ravine and begin plucking the shrieking motorists from the road.

That evening I learned that there had been fourteen kilometres of *coda* on the Italian side of the tunnel. We had sailed through and arrived on time.

A source of great delight is the common meal, though it is more common on the trains going north from Italy, when the Italian passengers have set out on the trip from their homes – that is, their kitchens. Italy is a country where, though the official religion might be Catholicism, the real religion is food. Influenced, no doubt, by the sacrament of Communion, Italians sense a moral, perhaps religious, obligation to offer food to anyone who is sitting with them when they eat. I have never been in a train carriage with an Italian who has not offered me part of whatever they are eating. If I refuse, they insist that I not be shy and have one or some or half of whatever it is. Or at least a taste: his mother made it, in which case the event really does partake of the sacramental.

And because I've come to believe that this offer is never an empty courtesy, I often accept, thus enriching my trips with all manner of fresh fruit, half sandwiches, large chunks of cheese. Often a glass of wine, or, once, fresh apple juice from the trees outside of Trento. And once, on the way to Italy, I found myself in a carriage with five Italians, and that demanded I open the box of Cru Sauvage and offer them round, did it not?

One curious phenomenon I encounter on the train is my own invisibility. This arises from the fact that I am a woman of a certain age, with white hair, who reads. Thus the customs inspectors walk past my carriage and fail absolutely to see me. They see young women, young men, anyone who looks like a non-European, anyone with a particularly large suitcase. But they do not see white-haired women who sit and read. I realize that I am perhaps abandoning all possibility of an interesting career in crime by failing to take advantage of my invisibility at the border. Well, there *is* that *parmigiano*, and there *is* that chocolate.

I much prefer to make the trip by train. Go to the station, get on the train, sit on the train, read, get off the train, be there. To go by plane instead requires a boat to Piazzale Roma, a bus to the airport, check-in, customs, security, wait, delay, fly, customs, wait for bag, get the train, be there. In the end, the difference is only a few hours, but the staccato rhythm of flying is not one that encourages the peace and tranquillity necessary for reading.

And there is the emotional and aesthetic difference. People on planes are usually grumpy and in a hurry; people on trains are patient and eager to chat. Airports are – let us tell the truth here – shopping malls where everything, from sunglasses to diapers, is sold at prices far higher than would be paid outside of the airport. Though I've been told that it is a beautiful thing to see a plane take off, I fail to understand why it is more beautiful than a bus pulling out of a bus stop.

As for beauty: clouds are, well, they're clouds, aren't they? And since I never want a window seat, what I see of the ground is limited to slices here and there. All right, all right, the approach to Venice (if you sit on the right side and have a window seat and it's a clear day) is spectacular. But so is the train trip, on either side, once we are beyond Como, going north and beginning to pass through those glorious Alps. Lakes, cows, sheep, more lakes, cataracts splashing down, and often beyond that, snow-covered peaks and the piercing blue of mountain skies that is unlike any blue I've ever seen.

And ahead, ahead is the mouth of the tunnel, that place where, even after all these tranquil years of easy passage, I can still hope that some adventure is about to begin.

27. Bees

I must have been fifty when I bought a house with a large garden in the Italian Dolomites, so I came to gardening late and almost against my will. I was interested in the mountains and not in the garden. My mother, however, had been a passionate gardener and had loved lilacs above all things, so I ordered some lilacs – only lilacs – believing that their magic power would transform the grassy field into a garden. When the package arrived, the lilac stems inside looked like wooden chopsticks that had spent too much time in the dishwasher: they were dry, thin to the point of emaciation, with tiny root threads sticking from one end.

It was early spring, so I dug four holes at random in the field behind the house, poured in some water, and stuck the chopsticks in, certain that they were not long for this world. Three weeks of spring rains followed,

and when I got to the house again I'd completely forgotten about the chop— er, lilacs. It wasn't until the
third day that I remembered them and went to see if
they were still there, only to find four chopsticks with
green leaves sprouting from them.

As stunned as Saul on the road to Damascus, I fell to
my knees to look at them, swept by my realization of
the truth of what my mother had for years told me:
gardens are proof of life's continuity, of survival and
renewal, and of the constancy of nature.

Since my conversion, the garden has grown as I dig
up more and more of the grassy field to create an ever-
expanding location for flowers and vegetables. Because
I don't know much about the formal theories of creating a garden, I plant what I like and where it seems it
will fit, and I mix flowers in with vegetables because I
think they look good together. A tomato plant growing next to yellow poppies looks pretty good to me, as
do asters among the zucchini.

As time passed, I began to get visitors: butterflies
and bees. As I knelt digging in the garden, I watched
them at their pollinating and soon came to realize that
they wanted to leave me alone as much as I wanted not
to disturb them. We got along fine. Curious to know
more about them, I visited the local beekeeper and
started to read, eager to learn what I could plant that
we'd all like to eat, and soon the garden was feeding
us all: luckily, they like carrots and onions, tomatoes,
currants, strawberries, pumpkins, and sunflowers. In
the springtime, the bees go mad for the blossoms on
the seven apple trees, and later in the year they delight
in the raspberries, as do I.

Paying closer attention to the bees, I realized how little I knew about them. Buzz, buzz, buzz and honey, but surely there had to be more than that.

Quicksand. That's what it's like: quicksand. I started out timidly, thinking I could tread my way lightly through a few books and come out knowing everything about bees; talk to the local beekeepers, even have a look inside the hives, and I'd be an expert. After all, how complicated could it be: they're only bees, aren't they?

As it turned out, no matter how much time I spent reading about bees and listening to people who studied them or raised them, there was no chance that I would ever understand their many perfections.

So fascinated had I become with bees that they had buzzed into the book I was working on, *Earthly Remains*, although I had no idea yet what their role would be. They pulled me into the mystery of their being.

This affects my work as a writer. If the book is about bees, even in some minor way, the characters in the book will talk about them, and at least one character will know a great deal about bees. And if I don't want to make a fool of myself, I must know enough to make that character convincing, which means both of us have to know a great deal about bees and sound absolutely convincing when we talk about them.

Quicksand is also an excellent metaphor for the wealth of information available about bees. Each new revelation of habits or genetics or lifespan filled me with amazement and led to greater curiosity. We've seen bees all our lives, haven't we, so of course we think we know about them. But I certainly didn't know that bees live only a month, nor did I know that the queen lays between 1,000 and 2,000 eggs – her own body weight – every day, every day, every day for three to five years, but what I most didn't know was that the hive, consisting of between 20,000 and 50,000 individual bees, appears to function as one mega-organism, each separate unit somehow tuned into the central function of the hive and thus somehow a participant in the decisions made by this multi-pieced organism.

Because I did not yet have any idea what part the bees would play in the novel, I didn't know what I had to know. Thus my reading had no goal. There was, as yet, no specific mystery to be solved about their behaviour, their intelligence, or their illnesses. I am in the middle of the swarm, surrounded by their buzzing, uncertain of what I have to learn about them or from them, but I am utterly without fear of them, filled only with interest, curiosity, and a growing awe at their perfection.

One obvious subject for any book about bees is the major danger faced by bees all over the world, something called CCD, colony collapse disorder. In springtime, when beekeepers go to check on their bees after the winter to see how they have fared during the cold and dark, some of them find dead bees on the floors of the hives, and even more find the numbers devastated, with as many as 80 per cent of the bees gone. Or all of them.

There has been no great scientific revelation of the single cause of this phenomenon, though the deaths have been written about in the press with sufficient frequency that most people know, however vaguely, that the bees are dying. If the bees go, it will be hard times for humankind: they pollinate as much as 70 per cent of flowering plants and 90 per cent of fruit trees on the planet, so their disappearance would take with them much of what humans eat, leaving cereals, which are wind-pollinated. More than one of the books I read contained a photo of farmers in south-west China, where bees have been virtually eliminated by current farming practices and the use of pesticides. (Remember, please, that bees are insects, and *pest*icides' kill insects.) The photo shows farmers who have climbed up into their pear trees, carefully pollinating the blossoms by hand.

Another example of what can happen when bee numbers decline is to be seen in the Central Valley of California, where 80 per cent of the world's almonds are grown. Because almonds require bees for pollination, in the absence of sufficient numbers of local bees (remember – *pest*icides?) the almond growers of the Central Valley import bees from other parts of the United States. Thus, in February, when the trees begin to blossom, 1.5 million bee colonies – about 60 per cent of the bee population of the United States – are trucked to California from places as far away as Florida to pollinate the trees. (One wonders how many Chinese farmers would have to be trucked to Central Valley to do the same job.)

Quite casually, one of the writers on the subject remarked that the stress from this migration is one of the major causes of colony collapse disorder. Nevertheless, off the bees go, sent about 6,000 kilometres, to fly free, from blossom to blossom, pollinating the almonds and thus saving the farmers, but worsening their own chances of survival at the same time. When the almonds are pollinated, the surviving bees are packed up again and back on the trucks they go, this time to be taken another 4,000 kilometres to the East Coast to pollinate crops that are beginning to blossom there. And when that's done, it's off again and back to Florida for the pollination of citrus fruit.

If you bear in mind that a bee lives only one month, you will realize that none of the original bees – save for the queens – makes it back alive to Florida.

Here we confront a philosophical quandary. Is a hive with very few original surviving members the same hive put on the truck at the beginning of the season? If more than 95 per cent of the original population is dead, is it the same population?

My guess is that the answer depends on the definition of 'hive'. If a hive is a group of bees with the same mother, who live in the same place as that mother, then it is the same hive, regardless of which individual bees are still alive inside it. They don't have the same father because, on her mating flight, the queen can have sex with more than twenty drones (all of whom die immediately as a direct result of their sexual contact with her) and thus the resulting bees, some of which are not fertilized and thus have no father at all, have in common only the queen as mother.

Now that there is, at least, a working definition of a hive, let me leave you with these puzzles about the function of the hive. Just what is the hive? What are the physical conditions inside it? What decisions does it make and who makes them, and why, and how? Who's in charge of things? How bleak is the future of bees and thus of humankind? What can be done to help them? And as a teaser question, I'd toss in this one: why does the queen preserve 6,000,000 sperm in her sperm reserve gland?

The inspiration was delivered by a friend who gave me a jar of honey of the palest yellow possible, saying that it was 'miele dalla barena' and had been made by honeybees in the Laguna di Venezia. And then ... well, I suppose I could say the heavens opened and the Muse descended on a gossamer cloud, pointed her magic wand at me, and said, 'Donna, there's your book.'

It's happened like that, effortlessly, in the past: an idea presents itself and a light goes off above my head, saying that the subject is worth a book, and so it has sometimes been; in this case, I was so sure it was the right subject that I started referring to it as 'the bee book'.

One of the obligations of any writer of fiction is that their discussion of fact seems effortlessly correct, as though all of the information about that subject had been in the writer's mind for years, and all they needed to do was consult their encyclopaedic knowledge in order to write about it. It doesn't have to be encyclopaedic, mind you; it simply has to *sound* as though it were.

In the past, I've spent months reading about diamonds and conflict diamonds, Chinese ceramics, art theft, glassmaking, rare books, and radiation sickness, and in each case, I, once a scholar, was kidnapped by the subject and ended up spending months reading about only that, to the exclusion of all other reading matter.

My friends have come to recognize the signs, and my social life suffers, for who wants to sit at dinner and listen to the symptoms of radiation poisoning or hear about the way dental floss is used to steal manuscripts? Only two months into the bee reading, already there were fewer invitations, and I had to listen to jokes about people who were abuzz to see me imitate the waggle dance of bees. A number of people, though only those with whom I spoke English, have started to call me 'honey'; others spoke of my 'stinging wit'.

I didn't quite reach the point of being the Bore at the Dinner Table, though I got very close to it. Nor did I start telling people on the vaporetto that bees have a positive electrical charge and flowers a negative charge that turns positive when a bee enters and takes pollen, thus creating a signal that will alert the next foraging bee (positively charged) that it need not waste energy on trying to get pollen from that blossom, at least not until it is again full of pollen and negatively charged.

Conversion to a religious or political faith might be like this, or falling in love: it becomes the only interesting topic, and other people must necessarily be as fascinated by it as I am, if only they would let me tell them about it. At the risk of making a fool of myself to anyone who really knows about bees (there is, after all, a universe to discover), let me mention some of the things that caught my interest and convinced me that bees are among the most complex and fascinating animals on the planet.

Their enemies first, all right? There's *Varroa destructor* – and doesn't the very name give you the creeps? – a peculiarly horrible-looking mite that feeds on bee larvae and can devastate hives; *Nosema apis*, a fungus; deformed wing virus; European foulbrood; and a host of other insects and diseases that can lay waste to the brood of growing larvae as well as to the short-lived adults.

Then there's man-made interference in all its manifestations: macro-agriculture demands the use of a cocktail of pesticides, herbicides, and fungicides, many of them harmful to honeybees. Are we surprised that their manufacturers insist that these products, many of them designed to kill insects, somehow manage to spare the honeybee, as if the Madonna of Medjugorje herself had intervened by spreading her blue cloak above them as protection?

The bees, at least for now, have managed to survive in the face of the many obstacles nature and man have placed in front of them. The hive lives, and in it one can see the perfection that nature can achieve if it's left alone for fifty million years or so to work things out. In the face of this perfection, one hardly knows where to start or what to mention. The rigorous class system is entirely based on the work each group performs. The queen results from a fertilized egg, deposited by another queen into one of the hexagonal wax cells in the hive and then fed on royal jelly; she emerges from her nursery cell a queen. She will eventually mate with many drones, themselves the products of unfertilized eggs that the previous queen deposited. These drone cells are one millimetre wider than the others. The queen senses their greater width as she crawls above and chooses not to fertilize these eggs, which will therefore result in drones. The workers are the result of fertilized eggs raised on normal brood food instead of royal jelly.

Worker bees emerge after three weeks in the cell, fully formed and itching to get to work. With a life-span of about one month, the worker bee will pass from task to task. She begins by keeping the hive clean, then she moves to the feeding of larvae, then to helping with food production, receiving the nectar brought back by bees that have been outside the hive to forage. Then she becomes a construction worker and builds the hexagonal wax cells that make up the hive. At twenty days of age, worker bees join the army and help defend the hive from invaders, and only when they've done that for a few days will they leave the hive to go and forage for pollen and nectar themselves. And then most of them die, exhausted and tattered of wing, worn out from work.

As I was reading all of this, I marveled at the predetermined order of it and at the way the hive seemed to be a single, thinking organism that received information, assessed it, and sent bees off to do the jobs that most needed doing at any given time.

One day, I left all the books behind on my desk and went to visit the bees, responding to the invitation of a friend who had invited me to come along and see his hives. We put on hats and veils, approached the hive, and found ourselves completely ignored, for the bees were far too busy to pay any attention to us.

My friend opened the hive and pulled out one of the wooden frames on which the bees had built their wax cells. It was crawling with hundreds, perhaps thousands, of bees. 'Do you see the queen?' he asked me.

I saw bees moving continually across the surface of the board, but none seemed more regal than the others. It was a brown mass, shimmering in the sun, flowing, glistening, in constant, slow turmoil.

'Look for the blue dot.' I looked, I stared, I hunted, I studied. I saw. There it was, a blue dot a bit bigger than the head of a pin: blue, fluorescent, on the back of her head, stuck there to indicate that she was a queen born in 2015.

She crawled slowly across the surface of the cell-covered board, pausing now and again to insert her hind section into the separate cells, where she lay a single white egg, about the size of the full stop at the end of this sentence. Beside her, above her, under her, crawled her court, touching her, embracing her, cleaning and feeding her, moving across her, for all I knew, cheering her on as she went about her business of producing 2,000 eggs a day.

I've never had a religious experience. I've never before had sympathy for that supra-physical entity Aristotle postulated in his writings on natural history, but to see her and to know even the minimal amount I learned in a few months of reading about bees is to suspect he knew what he was talking about when, failing to find the right word, he spoke of 'celestial is-ness'. Here is being, here is life, and here is as close to perfection as I've ever seen.

28. Tigger

Tigger is a thoroughly undistinguished brindle cat, grey and white, white spot under his chin, left ear clipped to show – in the visual language used by veterinarians in the canton of Graubünden – that he has been castrated. He appeared behind my home in the mountains some years ago, during the Year of Many Cats, and meekly took his place in the feeding line that formed at the door to the garden. There were, if memory serves, seven of them that year, with occasional visits from neighbours' cats, who had decided to come along to check out the menu at what quickly became a sort of backyard diner.

Year by year, the other cats fell victim to the merciless attrition of cold, snow, motorcycles, automobiles, martens, and, for all I know, foxes. Each spring there were fewer and fewer return appearances. Minnie (who bore a striking resemblance to Minnie Mouse),

Bruiser (who was big and had the aggressive stride of a boxer), Minnie Minnie (Minnie's baby), and Daphne (who turned out to be male) did not appear at spring's first dinner party; the decline continued until only faithful Tigger remained.

He still emerged, always within five minutes of my own arrival, but only if I'd been away for more than a few weeks. Either he'd made a home in the cellar or he'd had a computer chip installed under my skin. No matter what time I arrived, as soon as I set down my suitcase, Tigger was at the door: golden eyes alight at what I wanted to believe was recognition and affection but which I'm sure was no more than hunger.

It was no doubt the same computer chip that forced me to go and get half a cup of Brekkies and a cup of water with a bit of milk poured into it before I thought of anything else. He chose to remain outside, regardless of temperature, rain, snow, meteorite showers, or other inclemencies of the weather.

One morning in late fall, when I pushed open the door to the garden, I saw him in the napping hollow he'd made for himself under the first apple tree to the left of the door. He looked up, as he always did, but he did not leap up, as he also always did. He lay there, head partially raised, staring at me. I stared back, knowing something was wrong. I took a step towards him, and he tried to pull himself to his feet. And failed. I backed away and said soft, encouraging things to him, thinking of the motorcycles, the cars, the various predatory beasts that passed in the night.

I took another step towards him, and again he tried to get to his feet. I drove down to the veterinarian and explained the situation. Hopeless to try to capture a wild cat in a net because he would hurt himself even more struggling to escape. Nothing to do but try to give him some water and wait.

It was easy enough to fill a bowl with water and push it close to him with the end of a broom. He ignored it.

I went and explained things to the retired forest ranger, who knew him, I suspect, from also having fed him during the winters. He offered, not naming the method, to come the next day and put an end to his suffering. I declined his offer and went back to the house, where Tigger was still under the tree, raising his head enough to watch me pick raspberries.

That night, all I could do was say nighty-night to Tigger and go to bed, where I lay awake, waiting for the sound of a fox or marten and the last struggle. In the morning, I went out to see if he was still there.

He wasn't, and I chose to believe that whatever had happened, had happened quickly and painlessly, and Tigger had gone back into the great chain of being. Although I had never touched him, never gotten closer than the two-metre barrier of safety that experience had painted around him, he'd wormed his way into my heart. I missed him, missed the curiosity with which he watched me work in the garden, his company when I watered the plants, his failure, ever, to leave a dead bird on the grass outside the door. As a domestic animal, Tigger was a hopeless failure, but he was still a wonderful cat: independent, self-sufficient, polite.

Springtime came and no cats arrived. The food and water dishes stayed where they were, as if I were hoping to have another cat drift under the fence and discover that here was a place where the living was good.

One morning in April, suspiciously close to Easter, I came downstairs in the morning and glanced out the back door. And saw a brindle cat with a clipped left ear looking back at me. Not wanting to frighten him, I walked over to the door and saw him make the same double hop to the left and run to disappear into the cellar window. (Intentionally left open all winter. You never know.)

I filled a cup with Brekkies and then, barefoot, in pyjamas, shocked by the cold of the morning, I walked over to the usual place, poured them out and, as I'd been doing for years, turned around and said, in what I hoped was a normal, encouraging voice, 'Pip pip, tiddily pom,' the standard invitation to breakfast I'd used for years. Tigger hopped out of the cellar window, stood still until I'd moved back out of the two-metre range, and then bent his head over his breakfast.

29. Confessions of an American Handel Junkie

Decades ago, I had the great good fortune to meet, and then become a friend of, Alan Curtis, the American conductor and musicologist. We chatted, we laughed, and then we confessed: though Alan's name is linked with that of Monteverdi, he leaned across the table and whispered that Handel was his favorite composer. I sighed, much in the manner of the person who finds another true believer in the midst of the heathen.

Time passed, and we decided to proselytize, though we did not see it that way, not really. He had the orchestra, I knew the organizer of a music festival who was looking for two operas to present that summer, and together we found the singers. And all of it – the late-cancelling singers, the evenings spent in Diva Dienst, the singers bursting into tears during rehearsal – was

more glorious fun than either of us could possibly
have imagined at the beginning.

I am not a musician. I cannot read musical notation.
I don't know music theory. I am a camp follower, a
groupie, call it what you will: I am a pair of ears,
attached to a heart, that have listened to Handel's
music, to the near-total exclusion of other music, for
years. But – and I think this is an important but – I can
still be whammed by the music of others: Donizetti
makes me wild, a decent *Butterfly* reduces me to a
quivering jelly, and well-sung Mozart is almost always
sublime.

It is our great good fortune – and that plural includes
you, gentle reader, even if you don't know it – to live in
the era of the Handel revival. Fifty years ago, his operas
sat in libraries or in the scornful footnotes of musicolo-
gists. They were seldom performed or, when they
were, they were performed in the manner of the day,
which means badly, with the parts for castrati written
down an octave, with the resulting effects on
coloratura.

The plots – magical, irrational, absurd – were seen
as ridiculous in an age that preferred realism, even in
Hollywood films. And men singing with high voices?
Puh-leeze, darling; no one could *think* of such a thing.

But here we are, half a century later, in an age that
adores transgression, and who better to meet our
needs than Handel? Wild, unrealistic plots: Armida
arrives in a chariot drawn by dragons; can James Bond
beat that? Medea is carried off by two more: take *that*,
Harry Potter. A female character dresses up as a man
to try to seduce the new girlfriend away from the man

they both love. You want *transgression*? I once over-
heard a woman at the *prima* of *Il Trionfo del Tempo e del
Disinganno* at the Zurich Opera rejoicing that 'the evening was a triumph for lesbianism,' news which the
exclusively heterosexual cast greeted with a similar
bemusement.

Now that the music has been hoisted back up to
where Handel intended it to be, singers can again sing
long passages in a single breath, stunning audiences
with their virtuosity and – I've seen it happen, had it
happen – driving the listeners wild.

Some time ago, I had a number of experiences that
confirmed me in my Handelian faith. I was invited to
attend a performance of that jewel in the crown of
Wagnerian genius, that triumph of all musicality:
Tristan and Isolde. I went, and after a while the circumstances in which I found myself seemed strangely
familiar, though I had been to only one other Wagnerian
opera in my life. Was it the peculiarly earnest, one
might almost say joyless, audience? Was it the drone of
the music? Was it the composer's lack of sympathy for
the beauty of the singing voice?

It was not until the middle of the interminable second act that memory graced me: when I was teaching
in China in the late seventies, my students described
the Struggle Sessions they had attended during the
Cultural Revolution. There around me were the loyal
cadres, sitting joyless as the sound of the Chairman's
voice rang above them and around them. A higher
truth was being revealed, a vision of a finer life, passionate commitment to principles to which I dared not
aspire. All about me, dark destruction and passionate

excess was leading the way towards ineluctable death. There were glorious voices on offer that night, but why on earth did they have to sing *that*?

And then came illumination. It was not a Struggle Session. Nothing of the sort. It was, instead, the night at the local pub when the town drunk sat down beside me and started to tell the story of his long, tortured marriage. Up and down, years passed, good and bad, happy, sad, always wanting something better, something different, and listen to how he yearned and suffered. Yet never did he speak a simple, comprehensible sentence with subject, verb, direct object. At the end of the second hour of his story, I was still waiting for him to make some definite point worthy of remembering. But no, he had barely begun, and there was the whole long middle period to tell me, and then the third act to endure.

The very next day and the day after that – sure proof that the world is in the hands of beneficent powers – I was able to attend two three-hour rehearsals of Handel's *Semele*: very same theatre, some of the same musicians, but there the resemblance – oh praise the Lord in word and song – ended.

Whereas the first evening I had longed for a simple declarative sentence, Handel gave me an endless run of them: A, B, A. Say it, reflect upon it, say it again with elaboration. I thought of Wilkie Collins's advice about writing: 'Make 'em cry, make 'em laugh, make 'em wait.' Listening to Wagner the previous evening, I'd spent long hours feeling like the only sober person in a room full of drunks; worse, I'd emerged from the experience without a single bit of music stuck inside my ear, and I most decidedly did not want more.

Anyone possessed of a sober mind and a sense of fair play cannot, after reading through the libretto of *Tristan*, so much as whisper a word of criticism against Handel's libretti, least against that of *Semele*, written by William Congreve, one of the great dramatists of his age. Wagner chews over love and lust and obsession for more than three hours; Handel tells us everything we need to know in four words – 'Endless pleasure, endless love' – and he tells us with a tune that we are still trying to shake out of our ears in the shower the next morning.

Isolde tries our patience with her list of desires; Semele stands and delivers this: 'Oh no, I'll take no less than all in full excess.' Well, she is in love with Jupiter, isn't she, so perhaps we must allow her a bit of room for full excess? And Handel gives it to us in aria after head-spinning aria.

Perhaps it is those words, 'Endless pleasure, endless love,' that summon up Handel's musical genius. Like Dickens, he was a popular entertainer and thought of himself as such. He had no great theories, no great life concepts, did not see himself as the person destined to change the course of musical history. He was a workman who wanted to give endless pleasure to his public. He did so, at least for me and the other junkies, with effortless, endless skill.

When Handel's audience tired of Italian opera, he did not try to persuade them to remain faithful but switched his genius to the writing of religious oratorios, and into them he poured the same passion, the same joy, the same sense of loss. Only a stone could listen to *Messiah* and not believe.

He didn't have to take his public aside and explain to them about this leitmotif and that chord that would resonate then and then and then, or the alternating this and that, and *then* you'll finally hear how beautiful the music is. He turned out tunes, melodies, music that flowed in a seemingly – thank God – endless stream from his pen. His goal was to delight, and in his music one hears what a happy, happy man he was. His music, at least for unmusical me, is endlessly cheerful, and here only the English word will make it clear. Full of cheer. And full of glory and passion and sublimity and darkest tragedy, as well. But always cheer. He's given me endless pleasure, and I shall continue to give him what he deserves: endless love.

30. Miss Brill

I've often reread a short story by Katherine Mansfield called 'Miss Brill'. Miss Brill is an Englishwoman, unmarried, of a certain age, living in a small provincial French city in the early part of the twentieth century. She scrapes a living by teaching English to young children and reading to an old man. Her single joy in the week is to go to the public gardens and listen to the band concert, where she changes every unpleasant reality into cause for happiness.

The pathos – to some people, the horror – of the story is her final realization, after young people make fun of her and call her a 'stupid old thing', that she is a silly woman, and that she is old.

During the Covid lockdown, I was, fortunately, in Zurich, where I spent some months. Like many of you, I did the same walk every day: in my case, off to the Allmend to watch the dogs play and the frogs mate. Twice a week to the COOP for – well, for everything.

I had my Miss Brill moment – if I may call it that – in the COOP, as I stood in front of the self-checkout, scanning my salad and cheese. Behind me were an Italian-speaking woman and her two daughters. At one point, one of the kids got closer than a metre to me and the mother said, *'Attenzione, Claudia, una persona anziana ...* ' Like Miss Brill, I did not hear the rest of what the woman said. *'Anziana'* was sufficient. Good grief, I thought, *'anziana'.* Me? Well, I do see the face in the mirror every morning, but it's hardly *anziana,* at least not to me. I am not, however, to be considered a neutral judge of this matter.

But why my first surprise? And, stranger still, why did it trouble me to hear that word? In this case, *'anziana'* is no more critical than 'woman', is it? For the woman who used the word, it was description, definition; nothing more. For me, it was hardly a revelation: it was simply the truth.

On the way home, I thought about the remark and tried to understand why this word had so struck me: *'anziana'.*

Some years ago, the first spring day of working in the garden, I knelt down to pick up the hose lying in a circle on the floor of the barn, intending to carry it out to the garden. And lacked the strength to push myself to my feet. I couldn't have been more stunned if I'd been struck by lightning. For years, I'd easily picked it up, carried the whole thing here and there in the garden. But now it was suddenly too heavy for me to lift.

In that instant, I realized I'd become an old person during the winter. Here was proof: I could no longer do what had once been easy. The hose had not grown longer, nor had it gained weight during the winter; I was the one who had changed.

Of course, we often receive signs that things are changing, but they usually take place on our faces – the wrinkle that seems longer or deeper than it was the last time we noticed it – or the grey hair is now white. Or there is less hair. But those things do not affect our physical strength, so we can ignore them by simply ignoring the mirror, or by not wearing our glasses. Politeness prevents people from calling them to our attention, so on both sides thus is simple truth suppressed. We go on, telling ourselves we are unchanged.

But when we can't do something we once did with ease, we can't look away from it and pretend it didn't happen. It can be opening the can of cat food, turning on the water tap that someone younger and stronger has closed, pushing the lawnmower up that incline behind the roses. Perhaps we can force ourselves to do it, once or twice, but eventually we are faced with the reality that we're suddenly living in the body of an old person.

I thought about age categories and the way they can be used to discriminate among people. You can't do some things *before* you are of a certain age, usually eighteen: you can't marry, sign a contract, borrow money, get a drink, drive a car, buy a gun, buy cigarettes, vote. There's a clear legal threshold: do it when you're seventeen years and eleven months, and the law will step in to try to protect you: do it later, and no one will notice or care.

As we approach the other end of life, however, society washes its hands of us. Suddenly, there are no laws that will protect us from our own reckless choices. The same societies that do not hesitate to interfere in the private lives of people near the beginning of their lives refuse to accept responsibility when the same people are nearing the other end.

I've mentioned that adulthood begins at eighteen. At what age is a person ancient? What birthday is your last as a person of a certain age, after which you are 'anziana'? Which number changes your legal status? When does the law make you stop driving, drinking, getting married, voting? To the best of my knowledge, there are no such laws, perhaps because millennia of experience have shown that, however similar are the steps on the way to adulthood, there is no clear and determined path by which we pass beyond it, nor is that path necessarily the same for every person.

No one is surprised to see that some people can, by exercise and diet, grow stronger and enjoy good health, nor are they surprised to see that others, often through neglect, do not.

Those of you who are of 'a certain age' and have been moderating your habits in the last few years have learned that the decrepitude of age is not inevitable and that our bodies, regardless of their age, can still stay in shape with exercise and a careful diet. We will not become Wonder Woman, nor will we become Superman. Nor is it guaranteed that we will live longer. We will remain *anziani*, but we will be *anziani* with an increased likelihood of remaining healthy and strong. This is not magic, this is not wishful thinking. The statistical evidence shows, year after year, that the story of Miss Brill can change: we can make her drink her protein powder, eat her daily egg, her vegetables and wholegrain bread, a piece of fish or chicken, snack on an orange and a handful of berries, do her balance exercises and stretching, and then go and look in the mirror and say, 'Lookin' good, babe.'